D0191052

257=

Marx, Freud, and the Critique of Everyday Life

Marx, Freud, and the Critique of Everyday Life

Toward a Permanent Cultural Revolution

by Bruce Brown

Monthly Review Press
New York and London

Copyright © 1973 by Bruce Brown
All Rights Reserved

Library of Congress Cataloging in Publication Data

Brown, Bruce, 1944–
  Marx, Freud, and the critique of everyday life toward a
permanent cultural revolution.
  Includes bibliographical references.
  1. Revolutions. 2. Radicalism. I. Title. [DNLM: 1. Politics.
2. Psychology, Social.
HM283 B877m 1973]
HM281.B75   301.6′333   72–93460
ISBN 0–85345–280–6

First Printing

Monthly Review Press
116 West 14th Street, New York, N.Y. 10011
33/37 Moreland Street, London, E.C. 1

Manufactured in the United States of America

pour la liberté

Contents

1

Marxism, the New Left, and the Problematic of Everyday Life

Among those elements of the radical tradition to which the New Left throughout the West has been drawn in its search for an intellectual perspective and a politics appropriate to the tasks confronting the struggle for human liberation in the most advanced industrial societies of Europe and America, one of the most important has been that current of critical thought identified with writers like Wilhelm Reich, Erich Fromm, Herbert Marcuse and his colleagues in the Frankfurt School in Germany, and, to a lesser extent, with the Surrealist tradition in France and those revolutionary Marxists who, like Henri Lefebvre, have carried forth its original project in their work. Marcuse's influence on the New Left needs no documentation[1]—even if, to be completely candid, we must concede that while it has been profound, it may not have been quite so significant as the media would have us believe in dubbing him the intellectual "guru" of the student movement. Nevertheless, even in Italy he is widely read and hailed by revolutionary students as one of the "3 M's" (Marx-Mao-Marcuse). While the other Frankfurt Marxists— in particular Max Horkheimer and Theodor Adorno of Marcuse's generation and Jürgen Habermas of the younger generation—have, unlike Marcuse, disassociated themselves from the struggles of the student movement, they have nonetheless been of great importance to its intellectual formation in Germany and, now that their works are finally beginning to appear in English translation, may be expected to exert a significant influence on New Left intellectuals in the United States as well. The Surrealists and their continuators, such as the Situationists, although not yet especially influential among New Left circles in Germany, Italy, or America, were immensely important sources for the ideological and political development of the French New Left in the period immediately preceding the great events of May 1968. It was not for nothing, as Jean-Louis Houdebine has remarked, "that certain walls (always the same ones, in fact) during May 1968 were covered with 'surrealist' or 'surrealistic' slogans, attesting to the massive reactivation of this ideology." [2] Finally, and most recently, this revival of critical Marxism has revealed itself through the immense interest currently shown in the work of Wilhelm Reich. In France, where Reich had been practically unknown before the appearance, from 1967 onward, of a number of translations of works from his "Marxist period," there quickly developed a broad enthusiasm for his ideas—in fact, the inclusion of courses on Reich in the curriculum at Nanterre was one of the basic demands of the 22nd of March Movement in the days leading up to the May events. In Reich's own Germany, the revival of his thought (in the form of widely circulated pirate editions of previously inaccessible works) has been even more spectacular in its impact on the student movement and formed the basic ideological source for the experimental Communes I and II in Berlin. Only slightly later, an equally enthusiastic interest began to develop in the United States with the translation or reissue of Reich's writings in paperback form.

Although it is difficult to encompass the rich thought of writers like Marcuse, Reich, or the Surrealists within a single category, certain characteristic concerns and themes are shared by all of them. We can treat their ideas as complementary contributions within the broad framework of a common cultural revolutionary project which, in turn, accounts for their contemporary relevance and influence. Not only do they share a common determination to reconstitute Marxism *as a critique of everyday life,*[3] and a common interest in psychoanalysis as an indispensable instrument for this theoretical renovation, but they also partake of a common emancipatory project which has found itself belatedly reincarnated in the struggles of the New Left throughout the West. In this respect, it is not surprising that Reich, the Frankfurt Marxists, and the Surrealists should so strikingly have anticipated many of the central problems and concerns which have characterized the more recent movements which we identify with the New Left. Despite the huge historical gap separating the two "moments" in the history of the class struggle which produced these earlier theories of critical Marxism and the New Left in the 1960s, there remains a profound parallelism in both the situations and problems facing revolutionaries at either time and in the responses evoked by these circumstances. Although specifically concerned with the factors conditioning the development of the Marxism of Georg Lukács, Paul Breines has described the parallelism between the situation and action of revolutionary intellectuals in the 1920s and 1930s, and the struggles of the 1960s, in terms applicable to the writers mentioned above as well:

> In both instances the critique of capitalism originates in a "subjective" revolt against the universal poverty of existence (defined in cultural more than material terms . . .); initially defined and elaborated in idealist, existentialist, culture criticism concepts, consciousness in both cases pushes toward a new, coherent totalization of modern society; both move out against "Old Left" dogma and categories long surpassed by actual historical developments. . . . The historical situa-

tion in each case is characterized by organic crisis and motion within the existing order; at least for those with their eyes and ears open, *status quo* orthodoxies and habits are in a state of rapid dissolution. In the years surrounding World War I as in the 1960's, world history itself has broken through an immediately preceding revisionist and reformist period; class struggle and social contradictions have passed from latent to manifest expression; society is visibly dialectical and consciousness hurries to catch up. . . . [In both instances] historical-theoretical consciousness is critical and self-critical, prospectively revolutionary theory (knowledge of society as a whole and simultaneously the self-consciousness of world-transforming *praxis*) as opposed to "revolutionary" ideology (which seeks to legitimize a particular organization, sect, or state power). . . . In our view, the idealist, subjective, existentialist, culture criticism beginnings of revolutionary theory and activity stand, in both instances, as a vital stage in the life of the revolutionary spirit.[4]

What unites these two "moments" in the history of the class struggle and accounts for their remarkable parallelism? Probably the answer lies in the tendency for social relations and institutions to become "reified" during periods of relative stability;[5] that is, for transitory, historically specific relationships between people to take on the appearance of "natural facts," of eternal verities which simply express the way the world is, has always been, and always will be. In this way social roles and institutions take on an ontological status (the family, to take a typical example, "ceases to be a human enterprise and becomes a reenactment of prototypical actions founded, say, in the will of the gods, natural law, or human nature").[6] People who perceive the world through this mask of reification never question the exploitative and oppressive relationships which determine their lives, for they are unable to imagine that any alternative to this situation is possible. Only during periods in which the reifying structures of institutions are disrupted—during periods of profound social crisis and disintegration—does a clear perception of the true nature of a society and the structural relationships which characterize it become fully possible. Marx lived in one such period of political ferment and unprecedentedly rapid socioeconomic transformation, and he was able to discern more clearly the true nature of the social order he lived in—namely, competitive capitalism—than would have been possible for the generations immediately preceding or following his own, whose experience was characterized by a far more stable social environment. Since Marx's day, competitive capitalism has been replaced by a new type of capitalism, monopoly or corporate capitalism, which has developed its own, new forms of exploitation and oppression, masked in turn by new forms of reification and ideological mystification. What makes the experience of the 1920s and the 1960s so similar is that both periods represent times when the normally invisible or obscured nature of this new stage of capitalism have become "de-reified," and hence macroscopically visible as a result of profound social crisis—the former representing, in a sense, the birth trauma of the new capitalism and the latter, the initial manifestations of its death throes.

What the cultural revolutionaries of the 1920s and the New Left of the 1960s both perceived was that in comparison with laissez-faire capitalism—the capitalism of Marx's time, where the problematic of the human situation was expressed mainly in terms of economic exploitation and political oppression—the new type of capitalism contains an almost irresistable tendency toward the universalization of alienation. In other words, it tends to convert the "*totality* of social life and existence into an object of domination with the 'intention' of transforming all subjectivity and activity into reified objectivity" [7] (a process which previously had been more or less restricted to the sphere of market relations and had not penetrated private life) and of turning all human subjects into passive spectators of their own alienated existence. As a result of this process—involving the progressive integration of the social whole, the growing interpenetration of base and superstructure, and the increasing diminution of the individual's psychic space—it follows that, as (the young) Marcuse put it in 1932: "The situation of capitalism is not only a question of an economic or political crisis, but [is] a *catastrophe of the human essence*"—an insight which from the outset "condemns every merely economic or political reform to futility and unconditionally demands the catastrophic overthrow of the existing conditions through total revolution." [8] Inasmuch as the prerequisite for such a "global contestation" seems to be a clear recognition of the comprehensive and ubiquitous nature of alienation and oppression in the new system, it also follows that "the theoretical and practical critique of modern capitalism will be a critique of the *whole* or it will be nothing—but a repetition of the whole." [9]

Armed with these insights into the need for a contemporary theory of revolution to be comprehensive and anti-reductive,* the cultural revolutionaries began by criticizing the inadequacies and impoverishment of the Marxian tradition as it had been handed down to them by previous generations of revolutionaries. To be sure, Marx himself had sought to

---

* The conception of reduction as used in this book is that of Henri Lefebvre, who defines it as the tendency to take specialization to the limit, to divide labor and fragment activity, to treat problems in a narrowly analytical (as opposed to synthetic) manner, to isolate the spheres of labor, politics, and private life from one another. "To reduce," he writes, "means not only to simplify, schematize, dogmatize, and classify. It means also to arrest and to fix, to change the total into the partial while yet laying claim to totality through extrapolation; it means to transform totality into a closed circle. It means finally to abolish through the use of logic—without solving the conflicts and the awareness of contradiction." [10]

unite theory and practice, to reconcile thought and feeling, to overcome the separation between the personal and the political, but his original emancipatory thrust had been abandoned or diluted by most of his followers, who had reduced the complexity of his thought to a crudely mechanistic economic or sociological determinism.[11] In the theories of the Second International, Marxism became reduced to merely one of its elements, political economy, with the consequence that Marx's original notion of the dialectical interaction between base and superstructure became reduced to a one-sided notion of society as an economic mechanism of which all other phenomena—social groups, political institutions, and cultural products—were seen as mere derivative manifestations. According to this conception, socialist revolution would come about simply as a result of the inevitable development of the capitalist economy's inherent contradiction between productive forces and relations of production, to the point of the system's collapse. The leaders of the Third International, while criticizing such economistic perspectives as encouraging a fatalistic strategy of "waiting for the revolution," nonetheless tended to replace "economism" with an equally reductive voluntarism that simply turned economism on its head and, postulating the objective preconditions for the transition to socialism as already present, reduced the problems of revolution to a Machiavellian notion of political warfare. Whereas the Bolsheviks justly criticized the Social Democrats for neglecting the need for a specifically political struggle against state power, they themselves tended to comprehend only that aspect of state power which manifested itself as police power, as physically coercive force, and not the much more profound forms of ideological and cultural hegemony on which the state rested. They failed to grasp the necessity for the revolutionary process on the material and political level to be accompanied by a "reform of consciousness," such as the young Marx had called for, by which the proletariat would become "intellectually and emotionally emancipated from the existing system." As Lukács pointed out in 1922, "this emancipation does not take place mechanistically parallel to and simultaneously with economic developments"; rather, "it both anticipates these and is anticipated by them." [12] It follows that the struggle against political and economic power carried on by radical minorities only becomes truly revolutionary when accompanied by a simultaneous struggle for such a "reform of consciousness" within the masses.

The Bolsheviks' neglect of this dimension of the revolutionary process was partly and temporarily obscured by the extraordinary nature of the Russian situation, in that the ideological and cultural superstructures of the old regime were much less highly developed there than in the more advanced capitalist nations. But its broader consequences, only to be felt in Russia somewhat later, were already being made clear by the failure, despite a promising beginning, of the proletarian revolution to spread to the West in the years immediately following the Bolshevik triumph in Russia, and the subsequent success of the capitalist counteroffensive. This counteroffensive, provoked by the specter of 1917, was already beginning to consolidate its forces in the 1920s and has continued to advance through a series of metamorphoses right up to the present, crushing everything in its path. To be sure, the success of this capitalist counteroffensive in no way eliminated the objective contradictions of the system. On the contrary, the objective factors of the revolutionary situation have continued to mature, as predicted by Marxism, through the increased development of the productive forces to the point where bourgeois social relations have become a more and more obvious fetter upon their further growth. But while the capitalists failed to overcome the objective irrationalities of the system, they at the same time succeeded decisively in forestalling the development of a subjective consciousness in the masses of the nature of these irrationalities and the necessity of transcending them through the transition to a new mode of socioeconomic organization. In the absence of such a subjective coming-to-consciousness, revolutionary action proved impossible despite the presence of catastrophic economic crises. Why is the proletariat not revolutionary? Lukács asked in 1920. Because, he concluded, "even in the very midst of the death throes of capitalism, broad sections of the proletarian masses still feel that the state, the laws and the economy of the bourgeoisie are the only possible environment for them to exist in." [13] In the face of the masses' failure to achieve a rational consciousness of their own interests and to conquer power, despite their numerical and economic superiority to the bourgeoisie, the critical Marxists argued that it was necessary to reevaluate the traditional Marxist understanding of the relationship between the socioeconomic structure of society and the processes by which ideology and culture are formed. What were the processes through which the bourgeoisie, by virtue of its control over production and its economic domination over society, was also able to legitimate this economic domination by imposing parallel forms of ideological domination over society and within the consciousness of individuals, and hence to erect barriers to prevent the proletariat from becoming conscious of its interests and mission?

One consequence of this failure of Marxism to comprehend the subjective inhibitions to the development of class consciousness was to disarm the left in the face of the resurgent counter-revolution. As Ernst Bloch wrote in 1931, "The vulgar Marxists are not keeping sufficient watch on what is happening to primitive and utopian trends. The Nazis are already occupying this territory, and it will be an important one." [14] As a result of this failure to take account of the psychological factors underpinning the revolutionary process, Wilhelm Reich noted a few years later, a situation arose in 1932 where, despite the fact that at least thirty million Germans wanted socialism and nearly the whole country was anti-capitalistic, the victor was fascism, the savior of capitalism. Victory for the counter-revolution could not, according to Reich, be explained simply as a result of the manipulation of the masses by the ruling groups that controlled the media of public opinion and mass communication, nor could it be attributed simply to the betrayals of the bureaucratic and corrupt leadership of the traditional working-class parties—although both of these factors no doubt played a part in it. For the masses to fall prey to such brazen propaganda and to subordinate themselves to such a treacherous leadership must at least in part have been because this subordination corresponded to some deeply felt need on their part. It followed from this analysis of the fascist triumph—a triumph which would have been impossible had the masses' rational perception of their own economic interests been as effective as socialists had previously assumed—that it had become necessary to ask, with the great Hungarian poet and revolutionary Attila József: "So long as man's emotional powers—little as we know about them—are strong enough to enroll men in camps opposed to their human interest, how can we believe that, motivated by their economic judgment, they will devote themselves to the building of a new world?" [15] Such a question, however, could not be answered by a Marxism which reduced all subjective phenomena to the status of mere derivatives of socioeconomic processes, a sociological reductionism of which even the sophisticated Marxism of a Lukács seemed guilty to a certain extent. "By reduction and homogenization to purely *social* matter (a reduction that dominates in Lukács in spite of his will to totality)," noted Bloch in 1923, "one cannot adequately comprehend life." [16]

While the resurgent counter-revolution in the West was

demonstrating with a vengeance that was far from figurative the extent to which the maintenance of capitalist hegemony was based not simply on physical coercion or ideological mystification but also on an internalization of capitalist rule within the very structure of the personality—a factor ignored by classical Marxism—the degeneration of proletarian democracy during the late 1920s and the subsequent experience of Stalinism suggested that the attempt to create a new society on the basis of such a reductive, economistic Marxism could be as dangerous as the sickness which the revolution had hoped to cure. Although, to be sure, the cultural Marxists of the 1920s almost universally supported the Bolshevik revolution, they were troubled from the start by the tendency of Soviet Marxism to define the revolutionary project in the narrowest possible manner (i.e., as the replacement of the anarchy of the capitalist marketplace and the exploitation of labor by capital with rational planning of production and the collectivization of economic life). The cultural revolutionaries felt that such a conception, in which liberation was defined solely in terms of emancipation from economic exploitation, neglected the complex multi-dimensionality of human existence and hence of human needs. It failed to take account of the fact that besides economic exploitation and political oppression, the masses under class society were also the victims of specific forms of oppression on the psychological level, from which any true revolution could and must provide liberation. Rejecting the conception of *alienation* as developed by the young Marx,* Soviet

---

* Lefebvre, for example, has recalled that just as Western Marxists like himself were discovering Marx's early writings on alienation and were beginning to grasp the immense political import of this concept in the early 1930s, a series of events (e.g., the Great Depression and the inauguration of economic planning in the USSR) were tending to reinforce the tendencies of Communist orthodoxy in the opposite direction, toward economism. In particular, the dogmatists of "institu-

Marxism forfeited the profound insights which the application of that notion to the study of such problems as work,
consumption, or the situation of women, might have revealed. Thus, for instance, Soviet Marxism could offer
women emancipation in terms of overcoming their oppression on the economic plane as an especially exploited
section of the work force, but could not deal with all the
other (psychological, sexual, aesthetic, etc.) aspects of
women's oppression. Insofar as it even recognized the
existence of problems of this latter sort, economistic Marxism, by defining them as the residual and derivative effects of
capitalism, was able to deduce their actual or imminent
solution as following from the destruction of capitalism.
When groups like women or youth began to question this
simplistic equation, demanding that the revolution go
beyond mere economic reorganization to effect a more
complete liberation, it increasingly tended to be reasserted
by police power in the hands of an emerging bureaucratic
elite. The Marxist ideology, by recognizing only economic
needs as valid, subsequently came to serve as a convenient
means of legitimating the repression of any such extra-eco-
nomic demands on the part of the masses as might question
this elite's power. Having adapted itself in this manner to the
needs of the bureaucracy, economistic Marxism became an
almost perfect instrument of repression: every new usurpation could be represented as serving an abstractly conceived
collective interest, a "higher" interest within which all
particular or personal interests must be subordinated to a
common good—which of course becomes pure mystification

---

tional Marxism"—grasping that the hitherto disregarded concepts such as
alienation, praxis, the "total man," etc., not only provided an instrument
for uncovering numerous forms of alienation in bourgeois societies but
also might be used to expose new forms of ideological and political
alienation within the so-called socialist society—chose to reject the whole
approach of Marx's early writing rather than run such a risk.[17]

once all partial and individual interests are excluded from it.

Just as the abject capitulation of the proletarian movement in the West in the face of fascist counter-revolution
had demonstrated the bankruptcy of economistic distilla-
tions of Marxism, so also did the continuing degeneration of
Soviet democracy into Stalinist totalitarianism suggest certain conclusions about the nature and ends of the revolutionary process. The cultural revolutionaries of the 1920s and
1930s were the first to draw these conclusions; much more
recently they have been taken up and developed further by
the New Left. It was out of their reflections on these
experiences that the cultural revolutionaries were led increasingly to conclude that while the original project of Marxism
was a necessary condition for a modern revolutionary politics, it was not sufficient unto itself for this task. Inasmuch as
classical Marxism itself arose and worked out its concept of
socialism at a time when the old patterns of communal
solidarity and collective living characterizing pre-industrial
society were being destroyed by the bourgeois and industrial
revolutions and the egoism of a new capitalist class was
threatening to destroy the life of the many, it naturally
tended to give priority to the restoration of the rights of the
community as a whole over those of the individual. In
contrast, for the cultural revolutionaries as for the New Left
today, the experience of Stalinism—by showing that, as
David Cooper has put it, "revolution in the sense of the
socialist transformation of economic life and social forms
does not automatically entail changes in actual persons: the
same alienations carry over, the same murderous bureaucracy
continues" [18]—proved that any revolutionary movement
which simply aims at taking over the state apparatus and
effecting socialist changes in society without liberating the
individual psyche is, at best, a process of mass mystification
offering only a transient emotional catharsis to the masses
without any permanent reality of liberation, or, at worst,

simply an agency of newer and even more barbarous modes of repression masked by pseudo-populist mythology and rhetoric.

Any modern revolutionary politics worthy of the name must work from the start toward a broadened conception of the revolutionary project which can bridge this crippling disjunction between "liberation on the mass social level (i.e., liberation of whole classes in economic and political terms) and liberation on the level of the individual and the concrete groups in which he is directly engaged." [19] Herein lies a fundamental source of the great relevance of the cultural Marxists of the 1920s and 1930s for the New Left today: more than any other group of revolutionary thinkers (at least since the days of Fourier), it was they who most clearly grasped the necessity of overcoming the prevailing dichotomy between the personal and the political. Such a conception, they showed, did not abandon Marxism but rather sought to preserve and enrich its original radical core while integrating it within a larger dialectics capable of grasping and acting upon the fundamental events of our times in a way that comprehends their full originality.

Such an expanded dialectic, according to the cultural revolutionaries who accepted this analysis, had at the very minimum to fuse the critical economic consciousness of Marxism (that is, its grasp of the macro-dynamics of social and historical life) with a dynamic comprehension of the factors underlying everyday life and the forces conditioning the psychic development of the individual personality. Such a broadened perspective would restore the problems of the concrete individual to the central position they deserve alongside those of the collectivity and would facilitate the control by such concrete existential individuals over their everyday lives without external constraints. Only in this way could the revolutionary project be redefined so as to reestablish the identification of socialism with human freedom in the light of the further development of capitalism from its initial laissez-faire forms to its later monopolistic, bureaucratic forms, on the one hand, and the degeneration of attempts to construct socialism outside the advanced industrial world into forms of bureaucratic collectivism or state capitalism, on the other.

A number of currents tended to converge around this cultural revolutionary project of uniting the internal and external worlds, the personal and the political. As early as 1919, the Berlin Dadaists were seeking to reconcile aesthetic and political liberation. Their Manifesto of that year called for: (1) The international revolutionary union of all creative and intellectual men and women on the basis of radical communism; (2) the introduction of progressive unemployment through comprehensive mechanization of every field of activity; (3) the immediate expropriation of property and the communal feeding of all; and (4) the erection of cities of light and gardens which will belong to society as a whole and prepare men for a state of freedom.[20] Only a few years later their successors in France, the Surrealists, "offered their services to the Revolution," while affirming that the passage of power from the hands of the bourgeoisie into those of the proletariat had to be accompanied by a parallel process directed toward the emancipation of aesthetic forms and the liberation of the creative imagination.[21] In their view, the crisis of civilization demanded a total response, "an unbelievably radical revolution that would be truly extended to every domain." Toward this end, "all means must be used to destroy the ideas of family, nation and religion." "Transform the world, said Marx; Change life, said Rimbaud"; for André Breton and the Surrealists, "these two rallying-cries are but one." The Surrealists sought a method of cultural revolution based on a new conception of human possibilities and aimed at unlocking all the barriers, both physical and psychological, between the conscious and the unconscious, the inner world and the outer world, so as to create a *sur-realité* in which the real and the imaginary, thought and feeling, would fuse and dominate all of life. Such a praxis, aiming not at an abstract utopia but at the permanent unleashing of human creativity, began for the Surrealists with a series of very concrete liberations: all the faculties, tendencies, or elements that have been repressed, concealed, or perverted, must find release. According to this conception, desire, hope, and imagination are latent in all women and men and in their history; to become actualized, however, they must "have power." To give them that power—by liberating the unconscious, by placing creation at the disposal of everyone, by bringing imagination to power—thus became, for the Surrealists, the permanent aim of revolutionary activity. Only in this way, they argued, would it be possible to unlock the collective imagination of the masses, stifled by the repressive organization of everyday life, and the submerged creative impulse within every individual, whose suppression had hitherto been required by a civilization organized in the interests of repression.

Meanwhile in Central Europe, Wilhelm Reich[22] among others was searching for a new cultural revolutionary project based on their insights into the extent to which the forms of class domination imposed on the masses by repressive society were related to a parallel process of psychological and above all sexual repression imposed on individuals during primary socialization within the context of the patriarchal family. Class society was seen as producing the authoritarian personality type it needed to ensure its survival. At the same time, Reich argued that this psychological repression, while serving to perpetuate domination, also created explosive sources of conflict overlooked by Marxism—forces which might be utilized by a new cultural revolutionary movement in the interests of liberation, in order to help individuals overcome the authoritarian fixations which rendered them incapable of the social act of revolution. Reich argued that under the conditions of material scarcity that had characterized all previous historical eras, the libidinal energy of the vast majority of the people had necessarily been sublimated in the never ending struggle for survival. Now, however, this labor, this self-denial, has produced a level of technological development that makes future repression unnecessary. The result is an explosive collision between the claims of human instinct and a civilization that continues to deny them. Under these circumstances, the gratification of previously suppressed libidinal urges—pursued freely, in accordance with the individual's own need for creative personal development, rather than restricted by the need to reproduce class domination within the masses—will inevitably lead to an extension of the claim for gratification and happiness to other spheres of human existence. Just as sexual inhibition is a crucial component of inhibition in general, so also is sexual emancipation an essential stage in a general emancipation of humanity that will transcend capitalist society.

What both Reich and the Surrealists were attempting to do in their reformulations of the received tradition of revolutionary thought—Reich through an original synthesis of Freud and Marx, of psychoanalysis and socialism; the Surrealists through a less systematic but equally original unification of politics, psychology, anthropology, and art within a Marxism peculiarly their own—was to lay the intellectual foundations for a new definition of radical politics which would not only overcome the narrowness and insufficiency of Marxism we have examined, but also unite the struggles of the Marxist labor movement with those of certain newly radicalized or proletarianized forces which had hitherto remained outside that tradition. They were among the first to recognize the revolutionary potential contained within the crisis of everyday life throughout the West, as it was beginning to be revealed in the 1920s in the breakdown of the patriarchal family, of traditional sexual morality, and of old cultural patterns; in the emergence of struggles on the part of women and youth for greater independence; and in the search for new life-styles and forms of aesthetic experience.[23] Marxism, while still constituting an indispensable instrument for the critical comprehension of the crisis of capitalism as a socioeconomic system, had relatively little to say with regard to these crises of everyday life. As a consequence, it also had relatively little to say to those new forces of youth rebellion, feminism, cultural avant-gardism, which had sprung from these crises. It was only natural that cultural revolutionaries like Reich and Breton should have looked for additional sources of enlightenment which might complement the Marxian critique and, by thus extending its analytic power and its conceptual framework, facilitate the incorporation within its revolutionary project of the problematic posed by the new phenomena.

It was the truly radical nature of this new cultural revolutionary project which sealed its fate. For despite the cultural revolutionaries' affirmations of loyalty to the parties of the Marxist left, it was plain that the process of total liberation they sought to initiate not only challenged the narrowness of the traditional political-economic strategies of the left, but also the authority of the elites who had, in the name of the revolution, imposed their institutional hegemony over the proletarian movement. Unable to surmount the active hostility of these elites, the fate of the Surrealist impulse in France or of the German Sex-Pol movement inspired by Reich's theory was basically the same as that suffered by analogous groups in America during the same period. According to Paul Buhle and Carmen Morgan:

> Throughout the 1920–1940's, the Political Left intently and successfully stifled the personal liberatory attitudes of those in and around its circles of power. While the orthodox leaders of

the Debsian Socialist Party merely suspected (but tolerated) individual attitudes toward culture and sexuality, Communist leaders publicly forbade even the sexual liberation which Communist rank-and-filers practiced privately. Every effort to introduce a cultural component of any autonomy into revolutionary political activity was resisted by the Left as a whole in the name of a "proletariat" whom the leaders knew only abstractly.[24]

As a consequence of this repressive campaign marshaled against it by the entrenched bureaucracies of traditional left organizations, the cultural revolutionary project remained a mere utopian passion. Those who had originally been its spokesmen were either excluded from the organized left or else, like Lukács—as he admitted before his death—made a real or feigned self-criticism of their original position in order to avoid that expulsion from the party which had isolated so many of their intellectual contemporaries (for example, Karl Korsch) from political activity. Those, like the Frankfurt Marxists,[25] who remained true to their cultural revolutionary ideals, paid the price of commitment not only in political inactivity but also in an intellectual isolation that found expression in the inevitable tendency for their writing to become increasingly abstract and academic.

Nevertheless, if in the face of this isolation and "academization" during the three decades following its initial articulation—a period in which, as the basis for a new form of mass revolutionary movement, it was quite simply a political non-starter—this cultural revolutionary project cannot be said to have succeeded, neither can it be said to have totally failed. For, after having remained in abeyance for decades, the original cultural revolutionary project has recently been reincarnated in the emergence throughout the industrial West during the 1960s of a "new" left within which "the thrust and immanent meaning" of the initial project "has returned at a new level of vigor, clarity and concreteness." [26]

The development of this New Left shows that the further colonization of civil society by commodity relations and hierarchical power over the past three or four decades, with the subsequent intensification of the tendency toward the decomposition of everyday life—a tendency which was only just beginning to manifest itself in the 1920s—has made such a cultural revolution less and less a utopian desire and more and more an objective necessity. Even more strikingly, the rapid growth of the new radicalism has revealed that the potential social base for this project, more or less restricted to especially critical groupings of embattled intellectuals in the days of Reich and the Surrealists, has been vastly enlarged under contemporary capitalist conditions as an increasingly proletarianized population has discovered that its very survival, if no longer so directly threatened by purely quantitative problems of economic scarcity and instability, is ever more directly called into question by new problems related to the "quality of life," and by the obliteration of all autonomy by the universal extension of hierarchical power. From this perspective, it can be seen that the anti-authoritarian student movements, the so-called youth culture, the revolts of colonized minorities within the advanced industrial countries, the movement for female and sexual liberation, etc., all constitute potentially revolutionary responses to the totality of capitalist exploitation and oppression within their respective spheres. The politicization of these categories has meant that the cultural revolutionary project today permeates the consciousness of a whole generation and increasingly promises to assume the character of a mass movement in revolt against the world of reification and alienation.

It is in this light that we can appreciate the current revival of interest in the theoretical work of the original cultural revolutionaries on the part of increasing numbers of New Leftists. For far from being of mere academic interest, these currents of cultural Marxism represent nothing less than an earlier moment of our own situation. In this sense, the attempt by these cultural revolutionaries to synthesize Marxism and psychoanalysis reflected on the theoretical level the same concern which the New Left—as it emerged out of the silent alienation of the 1950s and the chilling horror of the nuclear arms race to confront the authoritarianism of existing institutions and the hypocrisy of a society which each day made a mockery of all the humanitarian and democratic ideals for which it claimed to stand—has come to express in its practice. In both cases, we have a recognition, born of profound cultural trauma, of the fundamental importance of defending the claims of the individual against the increasingly overwhelming power of a bureaucratic administrative apparatus which has fragmented all social activity and dissolved society into isolated individual monads. What was first enunciated on the basis of the original theoretical investigation undertaken by an earlier generation of cultural revolutionaries has been rediscovered by the New Left through a spontaneous dialectic of sentiment which has led it to seek to transform itself from an originally individualistic and emotional refusal into an organized refusal, and to launch a new subversive force based on the recognition that, as Max Horkheimer wrote in 1940, "the fully developed individual is the consummation of a fully developed society. The emancipation of the individual is not an emancipation from society, but the deliverance of society from atomization, an atomization that may reach its peak in periods of collectivization and mass culture." [27]

Although this tendency toward a fusion of struggles on the micro- and macro-social levels, of the personal and the political, is clearly implicit in the dynamics of the New Left's politicization, unfortunately it is still only a tendency, more a fervently desired goal than an accomplished fact. This is particularly true on the ideological and theoretical level, where the movement's initial distrust of and indifference to intellectual work, which to a certain extent was an asset ten or even five years ago, has become a crippling impediment to its further political development. Unable to bring together the different threads and currents of contestation within an adequate overall perspective and revolutionary strategy capable both of accounting for setbacks and incoherences and of discerning new openings and opportunities, the movement finds itself increasingly vulnerable to the manipulative techniques of divide and conquer, of containment and/or co-optation, by which the system seeks to suffocate potential opposition and repress consciousness of its contradictions. At present, the success of this repressive strategy is apparent, above all in the increasing difficulty of effecting the formerly much sought after fusion of personal and political on any level and the consequent growing disjunction between the two. At the height of the movement's initial burst of enthusiasm, during the late 1960s, it had seemed for a brief moment that anything was possible, that cultural and political radicalism were one and the same. But in the wake of repression and disappointed hopes, disillusionment set in and this unity was shattered, leaving political radicals with their ideological banners, their programs, and their organizations on one side, and cultural revolutionaries, convinced that all organized political work was a waste of time, on the other. In short, in Murray Bookchin's words, "the two sides became polarized into 'either . . . or' propositions as though oppression can be defined in only one of two ways: spiritual *or* material, psychic *or* economic, alienative *or* exploitative." [28]

The movement is presently in crisis. As the contradictions of advanced capitalism grow ever more intense, the profound inhumanity and moral bankruptcy of the system is revealed to ever greater numbers of people, but the New Left has no theory and strategy of cultural revolution capable of giving direction to this constantly enlarging fund of disaffection and revulsion. The movement's current fragmentation has brought disorientation and confusion, even despair. But to many it has also brought an increased awareness of the inadequacies of the forms of organization and activity developed in the 1960s. A search for new directions, new projects, new collective revolutionary identities appears to be beginning. Above all, there seems to be emerging a belated recognition of the crucial need to go beyond the recent "wars of quotation" between competing sects—which substitute textual exegesis from authorities ranging from Mao to Metesky for theoretical work—and, by reinstating distinctions between sloganeering and radical analysis, to inform spontaneity with conscious criticism and critical consciousness by rehabilitating the theoretical enterprise. Only in this way, it is becoming apparent, will it be possible to bridge the gap between political and cultural revolutionary currents within the movement and make explicit the emancipatory project which has already been implicitly posed by the New Left's practical development.

There has been an increasing recognition by many New Leftists that while they must avoid the traps represented by a fetishistic revival of what Marx called "the borrowed language" of the past through which "the tradition of all the dead generations weighs like a nightmare on the brain of the living," it is nonetheless necessary to base the elaboration of new revolutionary theory on a rediscovery of those currents of truly critical thought which embody the accumulated experience of many generations of past revolutionary struggles—just as it is necessary to base the actual resumption of revolutionary struggle on the reassertion and deepening "of all the old liberating endeavors" in the face of their incompletion or partial recuperation. Given this recognition of the extent to which the restoration of the link between theory and practice implies the repossession of the past, and a consciousness of the past in the act of shaping the future, it

follows that the preoccupation of more and more New
Leftists with the tradition of critical Marxism represented by
Reich, Marcuse, or the Frankfurt theorists, is no idle
diversion but is an integral precondition for the launching of
a new emancipatory praxis. Within the encounter between
this New Left and these currents of revolutionary thought,
we may discern the coexistence of a *criticism in actions* of
modern society, represented by the struggles of the New
Left, and the *theoretical critique* of repressive society,
represented by the critical intellectuals of the "Freudo-Marxist" school. Still separated but "advancing toward the same
reality and both talking of the same thing," these two parallel
critiques are "mutually explanatory, each being incompre-
hensible without the other." [29] Just as their separation to
date has seen the fragmentation of the New Left into a series
of uncoordinated and mutually exclusive currents of contestation whose existence is presently being placed in jeopardy
by their isolation in the face of repression, and by the
"academization" of critical theory in the absence of a
revolutionary subject capable of realizing its project, so the
unification of the two critiques may lay the basis for a
reintegration of the fragmented New Left forces into a
coherent revolutionary force, and hence for the reunification
of theory and practice into a revolutionary praxis uniting the
micro- and macro-social contexts, the transformation of
"inner reality" and "outer reality."

It follows that the examination of the critical Marxist
tradition which we are about to undertake is not a mere
exercise in revolutionary hagiography, but an attempt, albeit
modest and partial, to reappropriate our past and the
consciousness of that past, not in the sense of an academic
historicism which reduces thought to the genealogy of
its components, but in its connectedness with our own
historical situation, as an earlier moment of our consciousness of that situation and our own struggle to reappropriate

it. In short, it forms a key component, which must be both *preserved and surpassed*, in the new revolutionary synthesis which we must create if we are to make the future our own. Toward this end, this study will consider in turn the following basic questions:

1. The radical critique of psychoanalytic theory and practice and the attempt to dissociate the Freudian theory of instinct from its identification with the established social order.

2. The attempt to integrate the critical, anthropological core of Freud's psychoanalytic theory within an overall critical theory whose primary impulse is Marxism and whose fundamental object is a new totalization of the interrelations between the historical transformations of human nature and of social organization taking place within the framework established by the material life-processes in the course of society's struggle to establish its collective mastery over nature.

3. The mass-psychological basis of revolution and reaction in the era of monopoly capitalism: the crises of everyday life, of the family, and of sexuality as they relate to the failure of revolutionary democracy in the Soviet Union and the success of fascist reaction in the West.

4. Sexual politics and the struggle for the transformation of everyday life: Wilhelm Reich's theory of the cultural revolution as a fundamental prerequisite for social liberation.

5. The problematic of "repressive desublimation" and Marcuse's analysis of the "obsolescence of psychoanalysis" in the light of the post-World War II transformation of Western societies from earlier forms of "crisis capitalism" to the contemporary types of bureaucratic societies of manipulated consumption.

6. The emergence of the contemporary New Left and the search for a new cultural revolutionary project and a method

for the conscious transformation of everyday life under the present conditions of bureaucratic consumer capitalism.

Notes

1. Perhaps the best introduction to Marcuse's influence on the New Left can be found in Paul Breines' two essays, "Marcuse and the New Left in America," in *Antworten auf Herbert Marcuse*, ed. Jürgen Habermas (Frankfurt, 1968), and "From Guru to Spectre: Marcuse and the Implosion of the Movement," *Liberation*, vol. 15, no. 5 (July 1970). In addition, one might also consult in this respect Jean-Michel Palmier's *Présentation d'Herbert Marcuse* (Paris, 1969).

2. Jean-Louis Houdebine, "André Breton et la double ascendance du signe," *La Nouvelle Critique*, no. 31 (February 1970), p. 43. For a detailed discussion of the influence of surrealism on the May Movement, see the two chapters (7 and 8) by Pierre Gallisaires in Alfred Willener, *The Action Image of Society: On Cultural Politicization* (New York, 1970).

3. See Karl Klare, "The Critique of Everyday Life, Marxism, and the New Left," *Berkeley Journal of Sociology*, vol. 16 (1971–72).

4. Paul Breines, "Notes on Georg Lukács' 'The Old Culture and the New Culture,' " *Telos*, no. 5 (Spring 1970), pp. 7–8.

5. The *locus classicus* for any discussion of the concept of reification is Lukács' famous essay, "Reification and the Consciousness of the Proletariat," in his *History and Class Consciousness: Studies on Marxist Dialectics* (Cambridge, Mass., 1971), pp. 83–222. Important subsequent treatments of this concept include Lucien Goldmann's essay on the subject in his *Recherches dialectiques* (Paris, 1959), and Joseph Gabel, *La Fausse conscience* (Paris, 1962).

6. Peter Berger and Stanley Pullberg, "Reification and the Sociological Critique of Consciousness," *New Left Review*, no. 35 (January–February 1966), p. 67.

7. Breines, "Notes on Georg Lukacs," p. 15.

8. Herbert Marcuse, "Neue Quellen zur Grundlegung des histo-rischen Materialismus," in *Philosophie und Revolution: Auf-sätze von Herbert Marcuse* (Berlin, 1967), pp. 96–97.

9. Breines, "Notes on Georg Lukács," p. 15.

10. Henri Lefebvre, *The Explosion: Marxism and the French Upheaval* (New York, 1969), p. 28.

11. The best analyses of the roots and consequences of this tendency for Marxism to degenerate from emancipatory cri-tique into various forms of positivism remain Karl Korsch's 1923 essay, translated as *Marxism and Philosophy* (New York, 1970), and the various remarks addressed to this problem by Antonio Gramsci in his *Prison Notebooks*, especially the section in "Problems of Marxism." See Quintin Hoare and Geoffrey Nowell Smith, eds., *Selections from the Prison Notebooks of Antonio Gramsci* (New York, 1971).

12. Georg Lukács, "Legality and Illegality," in *History and Class Consciousness*, p. 257.

13. Ibid., p. 262.

14. In Ernst Bloch, *Erbschaft dieser Zeit*; quoted in Reimut Reiche, *Sexuality and Class Struggle* (New York, 1971), p. 18.

15. Quoted by Istvan Mészáros in his *Marx's Theory of Alienation* (London, 1970), p. 268. For an introduction to József's political thought, particularly as represented by his essay of 1932, "Hegel, Marx, and Freud," see Jean Rousselot, *Attila József 1905–1937: sa vie, son oeuvre* (Paris, 1958), and Andras Sandor's essay "Attila József," in *Tri-Quarterly*, no. 9 (Spring 1962).

16. See Ernst Bloch, "Aktualität und Utopie: Zu Lukács' 'Ge-schichte und Klassenbewusstsein,'" in his *Philosophische Auf-sätze zur Objectiven Phantasie* (Frankfurt, 1969); quoted by James Miller in his "Marxism and Subjectivity: Remarks on Georg Lukács and Existential Phenomenology," *Telos*, no. 6 (Fall 1970), p. 178.

17. See Henri Lefebvre, "Forward to the 5th Edition," *Dialectical Materialism* (London, 1968).

18. David Cooper, "Beyond Words," in David Cooper, ed., *To Free a Generation: Dialectics of Liberation* (New York, 1969), p. 197.

19. Cooper, "Introduction," in *To Free a Generation*, p. 9.
20. From Richard Huelsenbeck, *En Avant Dada: A History of Dadaism* (1920), quoted by Anson Rabinbach in *Telos*, no. 7 (Spring 1971), p. 141.
21. There is a vast literature relating to surrealism. For a basic introduction to the subject and a bibliography, see Maurice Nadeau, *The History of Surrealism* (New York, 1965).
22. Among the many works on Reich, I have found most useful: Constantin Sinelnikoff, *L'oeuvre de Wilhelm Reich*, 2 vols. (Paris, 1970); André Franklin, "Wilhelm Reich et l'économie sexuelle," *Arguments*, no. 4 (1960); Reimut Reiche, "Wilhelm Reich: Die Sexuelle Revolution," *Neue Kritik*, nos. 48–49 (August 1968); Maurice Brinton, *Authoritarian Conditioning, Sexual Repression and the Irrational in Politics*, Solidarity Pamphlet no. 33 (June 1970); Bertell Ollman, "Wilhelm Reich," in Dick Howard and Karl Klare, eds., *The Unknown Dimension: European Marxism Since Lenin* (New York, 1972).
23. See Christopher Lasch, *The New Radicalism in America: 1889–1963* (New York, 1965), and Martin J. Sklar, "On the Proletarian Revolution and the End of Political-Economic Society," *Radical America*, vol. 3, no. 3 (May–June 1969).
24. Paul Buhle and Carmen Morgan, "Notions of Youth Culture," *Radical America*, vol. 4, no. 6 (September–October 1970), p. 85.
25. Throughout this book, my discussion of the Frankfurt Marxists (especially Horkheimer, Adorno, and Marcuse) is particularly indebted to Martin Jay's study, *The Frankfurt School: An Intellectual History of the "Institut für Sozialforschung (1923–1950)*," Ph.D. dissertation, Harvard University, 1971, recently published in book form as *Dialectical Imagination*. Other useful treatments of the Frankfurt School and its influence include: Göran Therborn, "The Frankfurt School," *New Left Review*, no. 63 (September–October 1970); G.E. Rusconi, *La theoria critica della societa* (Bologna, 1968); Albrecht Wellmer, *Critical Theory of Society* (New York, 1971).
26. Breines, "Notes on Georg Lukács," p. 15.

27. Max Horkheimer, *The Eclipse of Reason* (New York, 1947), p. 135.

28. Murray Bookchin, "Youth Culture: An Anarcho-Communist View," in *Hip Culture: Six Essays on its Revolutionary Potential* (New York, 1970), p. 53.

29. "La déclin et la chute de l'économie spectaculaire-marchande," *Internationale Situationniste,* no. 10 (March 1966), p. 4.

2

Psychoanalysis and Revolutionary Thought

Having situated the currents of cultural revolutionary thought and struggle in the historical context of their development and in their relation to the contemporary problematic posed by the development of the New Left in the West, we may now, as a prelude to our ultimate objective of bringing this project up to date, examine their specific intellectual sources and content. We must begin by looking at why it was above all to psychoanalysis that the original cultural revolutionaries turned in order to remedy the demonstrated insufficiency of classical Marxism and provide the foundation for a new critical theory. With psychoanalysis under attack today from almost every side as an instrument of repression and enforced conformity, it is essential to appreciate the enormous attraction Freud's ideas had for earlier generations of cultural Marxists. We can begin by recalling the profoundly revolutionary character of psychoanalysis' original impulse and of its initial impact on Western culture; only in this way will it be possible for us to recognize the extent to which, despite all attempts to co-opt it for conservative ends, it retains a certain critical anthropological core indispensable to a revolutionary critique of contemporary civilization. Just as Darwin and Marx had absolutely revolutionized thinking about nature and society in the mid-nineteenth century, around 1920 people began, with good reason, to feel that with Sigmund Freud something critical had occurred in the history of human society.

Whereas with Marx human society became historically and sociologically self-conscious for the first time, it was with Freud that the parallel tendency toward a new self-knowledge of the individual, which had its roots in the romantic protest against industrial civilization, finally achieved the status of a science. To be sure, this tendency had already, with Nietzsche, begun to take the explicit form of a "psychology of exposure," illuminating the conscious awareness and rationalizations of individuals regarding the motives of their behavior actually constitute distortions and mystifications of their real motivations and desires. But while Nietzsche, on the basis of a historical critique of civilization, attributed this bad consciousness to the decadence which has been discernible since the advent of Christianity and which manifests itself in a psychology of self-denial and *ressentiment* that attempts to represent impotence and servility as ethical and ascetic ideals, Freud, in contrast, through individual psychological analyses, discovered the roots of this process of self-deception at a still deeper level, in the existence of an unconscious dimension to psychic life. As a result of this discovery and, flowing from it, the crucial insight into the possibility which self-reflection upon pathological compulsion afforded for the abolition of that compulsion, Freud was able at least implicitly to outline a method for psychoanalytic investigation which is simultaneously scientific *and* critical inasmuch as it establishes a dialectic between theory and practice at the very core of the therapeutic experience (e.g., the theoretical totalization of anthropological knowledge at the disposal of the analyst is reflected in the therapeutic practice which, by unlocking the reified structures of the patient's consciousness, elicts feedback in the form of new data regarding the patient's experience which must be decoded with the analyst's help in such a way as to unmask the patient's increasingly artful rationalizations and, finally, assimilated within the anthropological theory in order to facilitate the patient's ultimate totalization of his or her own experience). In contrast to all forms of positivistic science, psychoanalysis uniquely succeeds in incorporating methodological self-reflection into its method. It follows that Freud's psychoanalytic theory rediscovered and carried on the specific intent and self-conscious methodological ideal of critical theory in general as inaugurated in the nineteenth century by Hegel and, above all, by Marx. Within the overall project of enlightenment that has characterized the general development of critical thought over the last two centuries, Freud's distinctively modern appropriation of man's most intimate spiritual and emotional experience marked a decisive moment. With its emergence it became apparent that, as Alexander Mitscherlich puts it: "Man has developed a new function—that of acquiring an understanding of himself enabling him to control, guide and shape his actions—that puts the conscious into a dialectical relationship with older biological functions, the hereditary nature of which explains unconscious behavior which imposes itself as a matter of course." [1] As a consequence, it provided a crucial and hitherto missing component of the broader process of the historical self-formation of the human species, and of the emancipatory critique of this process which, by linking lost experiential dimensions of both individual and collective pasts, has as its project the unleashing of a transformed social parxis. [2]

It is not surprising, then, that in the 1920s revolutionary intellectuals like Reich, Breton, Attila József, and Karel Teige should have turned to psychoanalysis as an essential component of a more general revolutionary perspective. [3] They saw psychoanalysis, with its dynamic conception of mental life and of the development of the individual personality, as adding a new and vital dimension to the "unmasking revolution" begun by Marx in his critique of ideology. Starting from the discovery that neurotic symptoms, the irrationalities of everyday life and of dreams, have a meaning if an individual's conscious behavior is understood in relation to his/her unconscious psychic life, and that this relation between conscious behavior and unconscious life is one of conflict, Freud went on to formulate a dialectical approach to the study of mental life in terms of the conflicts, interactions, and mutual adjustments between instinctual drives and the claims of reality as expressed in social conditions and moral codes. His discovery that mental attitudes and behavior are rooted in conflicts and are, as a result, purposive—that there is, in other words, a certain subterranean logic, similar to Hegel's "cunning of reason," at the bottom of the individual's behavior that plans, directs, censors, and often deceives her or him—led him to the elaboration of a dialectical psychology which sees psychic life as the product of mental conflict, much as Marx's materialism sees historical life dialectically as the product of social conflict. As Arnold Hauser has pointed out, "the biological reality of instincts plays, in Freud's theory, a part similar to that of the economic reality of production in historical materialism; psychoanalysis is, like the Marxist philosophy of history, a materialistic . . . doctrine; it rests on biology as Marxism rests on economics." [4] Both theories clearly move on the same ground, conceiving men and women as physical/spiritual beings who are involved in a deadly struggle and have to engage all their faculties and abilities in maintaining a state of balance between the opposing powers that govern their lives. At the same time, Freud shares with Marx not only a dialectical approach but an emphasis on historicity as well. Just as Marx insisted upon the historical specificity of social systems and the need to understand institutions from the perspective of a genetic structuralism, the essential importance ascribed by Freud to the study of the individual patient's psychological history as the key to unravelling his/her personality structure is well known, as is also, and to an even greater degree, Freud's emphasis in his meta-psychological writings (*Totem and Taboo*, etc.) on the necessity of providing a historical explanation of a "global" sort for psychic phenomena (an emphasis which is in absolute contradiction to the so-called biologism and psychologism of some of his writings).[5] Finally, and again in much the same manner as Marxism, psychoanalysis offers a radical critique of the alienated society, rendering transparent the various reifying and mystifying structures—in the former case, of juridical legalism and in the latter case, of civilization—and revealing, as a central category common to both, the underlying realities of socioeconomic and psychosexual repression. To the socioeconomic critique of capitalism begun by Marx, psychoanalysis added an uncompromising attack on the traditional values of bourgeois society and its institutions, proclaiming the death of everything this society held sacred and reducing it to its unholy and irrational genesis. It offered an unparalleled instrument of liberation which not only eradicated a whole complex of inherited ideals, myths, and moral patterns, but which also, in opening the way for the exploration of the mysterious depths which determine man's behavior without regard to his conscious intentions, provided the basis for a new practice of individual self-enlightenment and creation.

Despite these exemplary beginnings, the psychoanalytic perspective contained a near fatal ambivalence which was later to allow its assimilation, in a form disinfected of most of its original critical character, into the very bourgeois civilization the full depths of whose oppressive nature it had been the first to reveal. At the root of this ambivalence was the fact that Freud's thought, although it derived its most profound insights largely from its dynamic character, also derived some of its worst shortcomings from the fact that it was, after all, not dynamic enough.[6] Although it has been asserted that Freud did not consider the instincts as immutable, it is indisputable that he maintained their "conservative nature" and conceived of them as changing so slowly that, in practice, they manifested an ahistorical, invariable character. Thus, in practice and to a considerable extent in its theory as well, orthodox psychoanalysis tends to treat the instincts and the whole biological constitution of the personality as being essentially static, and to see the constitution of the repressed impulses and the basic content of the unconscious as an unchangeable, invariable factor in human psychology—the so-called ineradicable animal nature of man. Similarly, infantile experiences and fixations remain, for orthodox Freudians, immutable and permanent influences on individual behavior which serve to determine, in an irreversible and insurmountable manner, even such later tendencies as the individual's inclination toward a particular mode of sexuality.

One more or less direct consequence of this tendency on the part of orthodox Freudians to treat human nature as essentially ahistorical and to mistake its present state for the human condition *per se*, was that the development of psychoanalytic thought and practice in the decades immediately preceding and following World War I was directed away from its original critical and subversive functions and toward an increasing accommodation to the existing social order and the dominant value system. Inasmuch as, in Freud's later writings and those of his orthodox followers, this ahistorical perspective led to the postulation of the destructive drives (the "death instincts") as biological facts which governed human fate in an inexorable manner, it inclined psychoanalysis toward a profoundly pessimistic evaluation of the possibilities for any human liberation from ignorance, slavery, and aggression, and toward an increasingly direct identification between the progress of civilization and the growth of repression. Against Marxists, who looked toward the eventual elimination of aggressiveness and instinctual repression as a result of the elimination of the structure of social exploitation and the conditions of material scarcity in which it is rooted, Freud argued in *Civilization and Its Discontents* that the development and preservation of civilization required the renunciation of pleasure and the regulation of instinctual drives, which is necessarily painful and repressive. At best, mankind could only hope to maintain a precarious tension between the repressive order and the productivity needed to sustain society, and the libidinal gratification and psychological freedom desired by the individual in this society. It followed that the revolutionary goals of socialists and anarchists were for Freud condemned in advance to remain forever mere utopian dreams:

> In abolishing private property, we deprive the human love of aggression of one of its instruments, certainly a strong one, though certainly not the strongest; but we have in no way altered the differences in power and influence which are misused by aggressiveness, nor have we altered anything in its nature. Aggressiveness was not created by property. It reigned almost without limit in primitive times, when property was still very scanty, and it already shows itself in the nursery almost before property has given up its primal, anal form; it forms the basis of every relation of affection and love among people. . . . If we do away with personal rights over material wealth, there still remains prerogative in the field of sexual relationships, which is bound to become the source of the strongest dislike and the most violent hostility among men who in other respects are on an equal footing. If we were to remove this factor, too, by allowing complete freedom of sexual life and thus abolishing the family, the germ-cell of civilization, we cannot, it is true, easily foresee what new paths the development of civilization could take; but one thing we

can expect, and that is that this indestructible feature of human nature will follow it there.[7]

Thus, Freud and his followers ultimately resigned themselves to the inevitability of repression. Unable to furnish a revolutionary praxis, Freudianism was forced to settle for a "reformist" practice of individual adaptation to a repressive order, refusing even to encourage sexual liberation. Once having made its peace with the established order by renouncing any interest in sociopolitical change, psychoanalysis found itself unable to resist further demands that it accommodate itself in one way or another to bourgeois morality. Initially charged by Freud with a fundamental critique of present-day society—and indeed, of all society—psychoanalysis has increasingly turned into the total antithesis of this original project, into a means for adapting individuals to the demands of an oppressive society. The analytic session has ceased to aim at a dissolution of the repressive powers internalized by the individual and has become a process of recuperation by which the patient, a victim of this repressive society, learns to accept her or his repressed condition.[8]

In the process, a psychoanalysis itself has become a mere ideology of the existing society, mystifying its oppressive nature and contributing to its reproduction. Shulamith Firestone has noted the irony that Freudianism, which originated at the same time as feminism and in response to largely the same realities (the decline of Victorian morality and the breakup of the extreme family-centeredness of that era), instead of becoming an instrument of awakening, capable of informing feminist practice, has become a powerful instrument for recuperating the feminist impulse. Particularly in America, Freudian therapy has been mobilized to stem the breach caused by the initial breakdown of patriarchal authority and, "regroomed for its new function of 'social adjustment,' was used to wipe up the feminist revolt." [9] Having subsumed feminism so effectively, it has become available for similar service as a substitute for Marxism, undermining the more general revolt of intellectuals against bourgeois civilization and values during the interwar years. As intellectuals moved from the barricades to the couch, the Marxist-oriented economic determinism so popular in the 1930s gave way to the quasi-Freudian psychological determinism of the 1940s and 1950s. No wonder that André Breton, writing in 1942, only three years after Freud's death, was moved to lament that his passing was "sufficient to render the future of psychoanalytic ideas problematic, and threatens once again to turn an exemplary instrument of liberation into an instrument of oppression." [10]

To be sure, this recuperation of psychoanalysis by repressive society was never complete. Institutionalized, dessicated, co-opted, Freudianism could never totally shed its original critical project, and so the possibility of rediscovering and developing this original impulse was at least latently present. Even within the Freudian camp, certain pressures toward such a revival and development of psychoanalysis' critical content were already manifesting themselves by the 1920s in response to the failure of orthodox theory and therapy or of the ever more diluted currents of Freudian revisionism to cope with the human problems generated by the post-World War I crisis of Western civilization. In the emergence of a new postwar generation of psychoanalysts like Wilhelm Reich, Erich Fromm, and Siegfried Bernfeld, we can discern a profound tendency, originating in the concrete problems they encountered in their clinical work with psychically ill individuals, to rediscover the radical implications of Freud's original conception of psychoanalysis' mission, while simultaneously attempting to free it from the ahistorical distortions which had served up to then to obscure the critical and sociological content latent within it.

"Psychoanalysis once worked at the roots of life," Reich remarked in 1937; "the fact that it did not become conscious of its social nature was the main factor in its catastrophic decline." [11] With the recognition of the suppressed social content of Freudianism, and of the consequences of this suppression, came the recognition of the means of making this suppressed inpulse manifest: that the renovation of psychoanalytic theory and practice requires the renovation and amplification of their critical functions, of their opposition to the prevailing forms of society and culture. Toward this end, this small group of radical psychoanalysts, this new "psychoanalytic left," criticized Freud and his more orthodox followers as being too bourgeois, too Victorian in their morality.[12] Not only was the standard Freudian notion of the analyst's role overly authoritarian, but Freud's celebrated moral relativism was based on a hypocritical tolerance, a specific instance of "bourgeois-liberal toleration." Behind the tolerant attitudes of analysts, they argued, lurked a concealed acquiescence to the social taboos of the bourgeois order. In contrast to this paternalistic notion of therapy, and following the lead of Sandor Ferenczi, Fromm and others affirmed the necessity of a positive rather than a negative relation of the analyst to the patient. This new conception of the analyst's role was to be characterized above all by an "unconditional affirmation of the patient's claim for happiness" and hence by the demand for the "liberation of morality from its tabooistic features." [13] At the same time, the pursuit of these ends—particularly for Wilhelm Reich—increasingly tended to call into question the whole notion of the "individual cure." It was becoming obvious that "the claim for happiness" only had a real substance and meaning inasmuch as it led to intensified conflict with a society whose organization and structure systematically negated such claims. In short, psychoanalysis ultimately had no authentic existence of its own outside a broader social and intellectual praxis of which it was but a moment.

In keeping with this commitment and in order to ground it in a theoretical appreciation of the possibilities for, and constraints on, its realization, it was necessary for this new psychoanalytic left to reformulate the old Freudian categories in such a way as to free them from their identification with the existing social order and to sharpen their comprehension of the connections between instinctual and socioeconomic structure. "Our psychological criticism of Freud," Reich asserted, began "with the clinical finding that the unconscious inferno is not anything absolute, eternal, or unalterable, that a certain social situation and development has created the character structure of today and is thus perpetuated." [14] The psychoanalytic left then went on to criticize Freud's attempt to give his assumption of the universality of the Oedipus complex an anthropological foundation. What his theory of the so-called "scientific myth of the Primal Father" really amounted to was simply what Norman O. Brown has termed the "postulation of male superiority and aggressiveness as an immutable fact of nature (the Primal Father, while the cause of culture, is in the state of nature) and the use of this assumption to explain the psychology of the human family." [15]

In contrast to this patricentric, authoritarian conception of culture, the left psychoanalysts turned to the theory of an initial matriarchal stage of social evolution which, as represented in the writings of anthropologists like Bachofen and Lewis Henry Morgan, was characterized by cooperation, permissiveness, and social egalitarianism.[16] In developing the argument, contrary to Freud's assumptions, that in fact matriarchy constituted the familial organization of "natural society"—corresponding to the era of primitive communism in the Marxian schema of social development—Reich in particular had occasion to refer to the revolutionary findings of the anthropologist Bronislaw Malinowski, who in his study of the Trobriand Islanders found no trace of the familiar Oedipal syndrome or of the customary mechanisms of libidinal suppression, repression, and sublimation.[17] Since social regulation of sexual life and reproduction was exercised among the Trobrianders by nonrepressive means, it followed that the phenomena of Oedipal repression and suppression must have definable and thus limited causes and functions. At least for Reich and Fromm, this suggested that the use of the repressive patriarchal system was necessary not so much in order to facilitate the development of civilization, but rather to create the psychological climate needed for the maintenance of class domination and exploitation. In short, sexual suppression is an essential instrument in the production of economic enslavement.[18] So long as economic conditions necessitate the domination of the majority by a minority, the repression of libidinal drives is necessary to adapt the psychic structure of the masses to this economic structure as one of the factors which lend stability to class relationships.

By introducing the concept of an original matricentric culture (regardless of the extent to which subsequent historical and anthropological research has objectively served to invalidate this theory), the psychoanalytic left took a crucial step forward in the development of psychoanalytic theory and in the assimilation of its critique of civilization as a product of instinctual repression within the Marxian critique of capitalist civilization. Inasmuch as it served to vitiate Freud's own identification of the "reality principle" with the demands of an eternal patricentric-acquisitive culture, it was able to suggest a reformulation of this concept in terms of a historical succession of different reality principles corresponding to the different collective results of the socialization of libidinal and aggressive impulses characteristic of the levels of development attained at various times in the process of interaction between man and nature, and to the resulting formation of needs appropriate to each particular level. It was possible, for instance, to formulate a reality principle specific to capitalist society. As Reich put it in 1927:

> To be concrete, the reality principle of the capitalist era imposes upon the proletarian a maximum limitation of his needs, while appealing to religious values such as modesty and humility. It also imposes a monogamous form of sexuality, etc. All this is founded on economic conditions: the ruling class has a reality principle which serves the perpetuation of its power. If the proletarian is brought up to accept this reality principle—if it is presented to him as absolutely valid (e.g., in the name of culture), this means an affirmation of the proletarian's exploitation and of capitalist society as a whole.[19]

To be sure, as Erich Fromm wrote in 1932, "the instinctual apparatus is in certain of its foundations a biological datum," but it is nevertheless subject to a high degree of modification through a "process of active and passive adaptation . . . to the socio-economic living conditions of the society." [20] In contrast to psychoanalytic ethnologists like Roheim, who traced the cultures of "primitive" peoples to their origins in a particular instinctual constellation and spoke, for example, of anal-sadistic cultures,[21] the left psychoanalysts tended to emphasize the extent to which the particular forms taken by a society's instinctual structures were shaped by social processes—most typically, in patriarchal civilizations, by the restriction of genitality and by the conditioning and intensification of the non-genital partial drives. The desire to accumulate which characterizes modern societies therefore has primarily a social origin, although, inasmuch as it becomes anchored in the psychic make-up of the members of these societies, it makes use of the anality that has been produced by sexual repression.

This recognition of the extent to which each historically specific order of society tends to produce a pattern of libidinous organization closely related to its socioeconomic structure was in sharp contrast to Freud's relatively ahistorical conception of the instinctual structure as a more or less static constellation of drives, and it was to encourage a reevaluation of the psychoanalytic understanding of the family as the central agency by which the dominant social order imprints its contours on the psychic make-up of the child. The left psychoanalysts agreed with Freud's identification of the family as both the principal arena in which the initial and decisive stages in the formation of the individual's personality take place and as the crucial locus for the transition from nature to culture—the Oedipal confrontation between the child and the father is not only the context in which the conflict between the individual and culture is first fought out, but is also the point of first engagement for the antagonistic forces of the instincts (that is, of those demands made upon the mind by virtue of its connection with the body) and of the claims of civilization in general. Inasmuch as the whole project inaugurated by Freud began with this basic insight into the manner in which the interactions and the disjunctions which occur between the different levels of psychic life are marked and to a significant extent determined by the familial milieu and the relations within it, it followed that the psychoanalytic approach to the origins of the personality had an implicitly sociological character. At the same time, in their preoccupation with the child's situation in relation to the family Freud and his orthodox followers had failed to grasp the societal extensions of these relations: from the point of view of orthodox psychoanalysis, "the adult is always a big child." [22] While psychoanalysis correctly revealed the relationships existing within the family in a particular type of society, its failure to extend this analysis to incorporate an understanding of the

broader social relations which precede these familial relations led to the confusion of these historically specific
relationships with an eternal and universal Oedipal confrontation. It also failed to recognize that the superego, whose
formation arises out of this confrontation, is nothing but an
internal reflection of society in general and of the principles
of authority which govern it. The "reality principle" which it
expresses likewise refers to the broader society in which the
familial environment exists, and all the inexorable facts that
frustrate, censor, or annihilate the pleasure-seeking individual
are social institutions and conventions whose cumulative
claims, commands threats, and sanctions are the principal
patrimony which the family in its "civilizing" zeal bequeaths
to the child.

It is above all through the family, then, that society
generates neuroses via its basic institutions and anchors itself
in the individual personality. And it follows that the connections between family members which mark the child's future
growth are social relationships which not only structure the
family as a discrete social group, but which also constitute
extensions of broader societal relationships which precede
these familial relations. The formalistic parallel drawn by
orthodox Freudians between the helplessness of the small
child in the family and of the adult in the face of naturalistic
social forces was invalid. As Fromm pointed out, it is not the
biological helplessness of the infant which is the decisive
factor in its specific need for a definite form of authority; it is
the social helplessness of the adult, determined by his or her
subordination to the dominant forms of socioeconomic
organization, which molds the concrete manifestations of the
child's biological helplessness and in this way influences the
form taken by the development of authority in the child.
The psychoanalytic critique of the family, it follows, contains
an implicit sociology; the familial institution, whose domination leaves its mark on the child's future development

by planting the seeds of neurosis, is itself marked by the structure of domination in the society at large which it functions to transmit.[23]

When this micro-sociological understanding of familial life is divorced from its broader social context and hypostatized, as in most orthodox Freudian literature, in the form of an ahistorical conceptualization (i.e., as a universally monogamous, patriarchal, precariously balanced institution within which the same Oedipal drama is forever being repeated, irrespective of the forces that modify its character over the course of time), the psychoanalytic perspective loses all meaning and substance. It follows that this psychoanalytic micro-sociology is only valid to the extent that it is integrated within a macro-sociological analysis, such as Marxism, capable of explicating the dialectical relationship between family and society in history. As Althusser puts it:

> The discussion of the forms of *familial ideology* and the crucial role they play in initiating the functioning of the instance that Freud called "the unconscious" . . . (e.g., the ideology of paternity-maternity-conjugality-infancy and their interrelations) is crucial, for it implies the conclusion . . . that *no theory of psychoanalysis can be produced without basing it on historical materialism* (on which the theory of the formations of familial ideology depends, in the last instance).[24]

It is only in the analysis of the history of this familial institution in its dialectical relationship to the history of society and culture as a whole that it becomes possible to understand the complex interrelationship between the world-historical process of socioeconomic and political development leading up to present-day repressive society and the socialization process underlying the development of the repressed personality of today. In this regard it is useful to recall the neglected insight of Frederick Engels into the importance of understanding familial relations as an essential element of what Marx called relations of production:

> According to the materialistic conception, the determining factor in history is, in the final instance, the production and reproduction of the immediate essentials of life. This is of a twofold character. On the one side, the production of the means of existence, of articles of food and clothing, dwellings, and of the tools necessary for that production; on the other side, the production of human beings themselves. The social organization under which the people of a particular historical epoch and a particular country live is determined by both kinds of production: by the stage of the development of labor on the one hand, and of the family on the other.[25]

Although in relatively primitive agrarian societies there tended to be a correspondence between familial organization and economic organization, with the growth of the productive forces, the increasing complexity of the division of labor, and the growing separation between production and consumption, these two spheres have become ever more separate. Under capitalism, the separation between public and private, between work and home, and between society and the individual, conceals the coexistence of two systems of domination. On the one hand, there is the system of material production characterized by the dominance of the bourgeoisie and the exploitation of the proletariat; on the other hand, there is the familial system characterized by patriarchal domination and the oppression of women and children. According to the Freudo-Marxists, Marx and Engels understood the economic functions which the system of patriarchal domination performed vis-à-vis the dominant class system, but, lacking an adequate psychological perspective, overlooked its even more crucial social and political function in the reproduction of class society. As Reich put it:

> In the pre-capitalistic phase of home industry and in early industrial capitalism, the family had immediate roots in the

familial economy . . . With the development of the means of production and the collectivization of the work process, however, there occurred *a change in the function of the family*. Its immediate economic basis became less significant to the extent to which the woman was included in the productive process; its place was taken by the *political function* which the family now began to assume. Its cardinal function, that for which it is mostly supported and defended by conservative science and law, is that of serving as *a factory for authoritarian ideologies* and conservative [mental] structures. It forms the educational apparatus through which practically every individual of our society, from the moment of drawing his first breath, has to pass. It influences the child in the sense of a reactionary ideology not only as an authoritarian institution, but also on the strength of its own structure; it is the conveyor belt between the economic structure of conservative society and its ideological superstructure; its reactionary atmosphere must needs become inextricably implanted in every one of its members.[26]

For Reich and the Freudo-Marxists, then, inasmuch as modern society is based to a significant degree on specific psychic attitudes which are partially rooted in unconscious drives and which serve as an effective complement to the external coerciveness of the dominant class system, the patriarchal family, in addition to its economic functions, also constitutes one of the most important loci for producing in individuals the psychic structure necessary to maintain the stability of the existing class society. This repressive function of the family—as Reich showed and as was documented empirically by the various investigators (Erich Fromm, Max Horkheimer, etc.) who compiled the Frankfurt School's voluminous collection, *Studien über Autorität und Familie*[27]—is first of all exercised through the relationship between the wife and children and the patriarchal father, who functions to a greater or lesser extent as "the exponent and representative of the authority of the state in the family." As regards the typical structure which Reich calls "the middle-class family"—but which he sees as extending far beyond the objective limits of that particular class into the upper classes and into the working class—the father, "because of the contradiction between his position in the production process (subordinate) and his family function (boss), . . . is a top-sergeant type; he kotows to those above, absorbs the prevailing attitudes (hence his tendency to imitation) and dominates those below; [finally,] he transmits the [prevailing] governmental and social concepts and enforces them." [28]

In addition to making this *sociological* analysis of the extent to which the patriarchal structure of familial life is bound up with the class character of society, the Freudo-Marxists also went on to reexamine, in the context of this broadened perspective, the specifically *psychological* foundations of the patriarchal family. Here the major emphasis of their investigations was on the role played by the repression of childhood creativity in general, and of infantile sexuality in particular, in stifling the spontaneous development of the child's personality and in rendering it generally susceptible to the process of repressive socialization by which external forms of domination are "imprinted" on the individual's character. In this regard:

> The repression of sexual needs creates a general weakening of intellectual and emotional functioning; in particular, it makes people lack [a capacity for] independence, will-power and critical faculties. . . . [In this way, the compulsive, patriarchal family, through] the anchoring of sexual morality and the changes it brings about in the organism create that specific psychic structure which forms the mass-psychological basis of any authoritarian social order. The vassel-structure is a mixture of sexual impotence, helplessness, longing for a Führer, fear of authority, fear of life, and mysticism. . . . Fear of sexuality and sexual hypocrisy characterize the "Babbitt" and his milieu. People with such a structure are incapable of democratic living.[29]

It is clear that the process of individual repression and neurosis-formation, carried on within the patriarchal family in line with repressive society's constant need to suppress the child's libidinal and creative development, and endowing the child with a permanent sense of guilt and inhibition without which he or she would never submit to authority, becomes an essential instrument of later social, economic, and political enslavement. "The psychological and sexual suffering of children," to quote Reich, "is the very first consequence of sexual repression by the parents, to which is later added the intellectual repression of the school, the spiritual brutalization of the church, and finally the oppression and material exploitation of the bosses." [30] Respect for authority in general, for law and order and the state, all ultimately depend on the success of parents in subordinating their children and on the specific psychological mutilation and generalized inhibitions induced by the process of repressive socialization. The family serves this psychosocial function, according to Fromm, by producing that typical emotional complex which he describes as the "patricentric" complex. It characteristically includes the following traits:

> Affective dependence on fatherly authority involving a mixture of anxiety, love and hate; identification with paternal authority vis-à-vis weaker ones; a strong and strict superego whose principle is that duty is more important than happiness; guilt feelings, reproduced over and over again by the discrepancy between the demands of the superego and those of reality whose effect is to keep people docile to authority. [31]

It was therefore "no accident that psychoanalysis was first conceived in the context of private life, of family conflicts, economically speaking in the sphere of consumption," [32] for independently of its economic functions it is in the familial context that the specifically psychological play of forces is found through which the larger social order defines and creates the type of personality that is necessary to the frictionless operation and reproduction of that society. Although the whole of society's institutional apparatus ultimately collaborates in ensuring the success of this process of repressive socialization, it is upon the efficacy of the initial stages of this operation, carried on, above all, within the familial environment, that the whole endeavor depends. Inasmuch as "the totality of relationships in the present age, the universal web of things, was strengthened and stabilized by one particular element—namely authority—and the process of strengthening and stabilization went on essentially at the particular, concrete level of the family," it follows that "the family was the 'germ cell' of bourgeois culture." [33] It is, for example, primarily due to the fact that certain cultural forms or ideologies are rooted in the affective framework constituted by the psychosocial syndrome of the patriarchal family, monogamous marriage, and sexual repression, that we can account for their tenacity despite their apparent obsolescence vis-à-vis socioeconomic development. "To the extent that they consist not of customs and interests more or less closely connected with material existence, but of so-called spiritual ideas, they have no independent reality," [34] but rather derive their tenacity from the fact that they correspond to the deeply felt emotional and motivational patterns which have become standardized in groups and individuals as a consequence of their situation and history, and which determine how such groups will react to socioeconomic changes. It is within the analysis of how these patterns constituting the psychic make-up of groups and individuals act to "cement" the culture of a particular epoch together that it becomes possible to account for the celebrated phenomenon of "cultural lag"—the disjuncture which typically arises in the historical process between the objective transformation of social and economic processes and the subjective modes through which men and women respond to these transformations at any particular point in time.

Finally, in addition to demonstrating the extent to which repressive sexual morality, within the contest of the patriarchal family, and the formation of a compulsive character structure were essential supports for a repressive social order, this Freudo-Marxist perspective, as developed by Reich, Fromm, and Horkheimer, also revealed how these characterological processes created specific contradictions which might under the proper conditions serve a progressive and even revolutionary function instead of their customary conservative one. Despite the fact that all the characterological traits of the repressed individual have developed in an intimate connection with coercion and necessities of various kinds and are, as Horkheimer has argued, "largely to be understood as interiorized force, as external law taken into the psyche itself, . . . in the psychic economy of the individual they are in the last analysis specific powers which lead men not only to accept existing conditions, but also at times to oppose them." [35] Such a Freudo-Marxist perspective views

> cultural arrangements and processes, in all areas of life, insofar as they influence the character and behavior of men at all [as either] conservative or disruptive factors in the dynamics of society: either they provide the mortar of the building under construction, the cement which artificially holds together the parts that tend toward independence, or they are part of the forces which will destroy the society.[36]

From this perspective, sexual repression, for example, is revealed not only as a factor serving to strengthen every kind of authoritarian rule—above all through instilling in youth a character structure tending toward compulsive submission to authority—but also as a force which may simultaneously undermine the authoritarian order through the sexual misery it produces—in particular, for Reich, by generating the sexual rebellion of youth. "Social sexual repression thus undermines itself by generating a steadily growing divergence between the tension of sexual needs and the external possibility of and internal capacity for gratification." [37] Should such a "sexual crisis" occur in conjunction with the growth of the objective contradictions within the existing society and the disintegration of existing class relations, libidinal energies would become freed for new uses and new social functions: "They no longer [would] serve the preservation of the society, but [would] contribute to the development of new social formations—they [would] cease to be 'cement' and turn into dynamite." [38] As Fromm put it in 1934, when his position was still in substantial agreement with that of Reich:

> Sexuality offers one of the most elementary and powerful opportunities for satisfaction and happiness. If it were permitted to the full extent required for the productive development of the human personality, rather than limited by the need to maintain control over the masses, the fulfillment of this important opportunity for happiness would necessarily lead to intensified demands for satisfaction and happiness in other areas of life. Since the satisfaction of these further demands would have to be achieved through material means, these demands of themselves would lead to the breakup of the existing social order. [39]

It followed that although Freud's fear of the "sexual chaos" that would result from the release of repressed instinctive drives from the restraints of civilized morality was justified, this phenomenon is nonetheless specific to a definite historical period, that of a class society. Under different social conditions, Reich insisted, on the basis of insights first culled from his therapeutic work, "a different regulation of social living . . . [would be] possible." [40]

Out of this path-breaking attempt by the first generation of Freudo-Marxists to link the psychoanalytic theory of repression with that of its abolition, the full depth of the psychoanalytic critique and the extent to which it transcends the existing order was at last revealed. From this recognition of psychoanalysis' social nature, of the need to free it from the ahistorical distortion of Freud's reactionary cultural philosophy, and of the essential relationship between forms of psychosexual repression and the development of modes of socioeconomic exploitation, there followed certain crucial practical and theoretical necessities. In the first place, just as sexual suppression is an essential instrument of economic enslavement, so also is the struggle for psychosexual emancipation an essential aspect of the general struggle for human liberation leading beyond repressive civilization in general and capitalist society in particular. Psychoanalysis, through its analysis of psychic misery, of the relation between this misery and the family, and of its source in sexual repression, shows that the solution to this misery demands both the abolition of the patriarchal family and the development of new means for the collective upbringing and education of children. Certain themes of this psychoanalytically based sexual sociology converged with political psychology to demonstrate that any authoritarian society—and especially capitalist society—is necessarily based on sexual repression and that, as a consequence, the sexual revolution which is necessary to do away with psychic misery is also an essential prerequisite for the abolition of social oppression.

In the second place, by demonstrating that the actualization of the psychoanalytic project through the liberation of repressed instinctual drives cannot be divorced from the broader question of social revolution, it was shown that further deepening of the social content of psychoanalytical concepts and sharpening of their critical function was possible only through their integration within the broader analysis of society as a whole provided by historical materialism—an alliance which psychoanalysis is all the more suited to enter into inasmuch as it is itself critical and revolutionary in many of its aspects:

Clearly, analytic psychology has its place within the framework of historical materialism. It investigates one of the natural factors that is operative in the relationship between society and nature: the realm of human drives, and the active and passive role they play within the social process. Thus it investigates a factor that plays a decisive mediating role between the economic base and the formation of ideologies. Thus, analytic social psychology enables us to understand fully the ideological superstructure in terms of the process that goes on between society and man's nature. Now we can readily summarize the findings of our study on the method and function of a psychoanalytic social psychology. Its method is that of classical Freudian psychoanalysis as applied to social phenomena. It explains the shared, socially relevant psychic attitudes in terms of the process of active and passive adaptation of the apparatus of drives to the socio-economic living conditions of the society. Its task is, first of all, to analyze the socially relevant libidinal strivings, i.e., to describe the libidinal structure of a given society and to explain the origin of this structure and its function in the social process.[41] *

---

* While this formulation by Fromm of the role of psychoanalysis vis-à-vis historical materialism was in most respects very close to that of Reich and was, with somewhat greater qualification, also indicative of the thinking of the other Frankfurt Marxists at that time, it should be noted that during the ensuing decade Fromm moved increasingly away from these positions toward both a rejection of libido theory altogether and a more conservative view of sexuality. Accordingly, he was criticized, first by Horkheimer and subsequently by Adorno and Marcuse, for attempting to collapse psychology into sociology and, by desexualizing psychology, to turn it into an instrument of social adaptation. "Psychology without libido," wrote Horkheimer in a letter to Leo Lowenthal (dated October 31, 1942, and quoted in Martin Jay's dissertation), "is in a way no

At the same time, however, the recognition of the necessity for such a synthesis in no way eliminated certain formidable obstacles and problems standing in the way of its actualization. Despite the fact that the fundamental, if implicit, logic underlying the internal development of both currents of thought was manifesting itself in the mutual attraction between the two, any attempt at actually effecting this liaison between Marxian "historicism" and Freudian "psychologism" or "biologism" was invariably greeted by the unmitigated hostility of "official" spokesmen and guardians of orthodoxy on either side.[42] Although a budding psychoanalytical movement began to emerge in Russia in the early 1920s, in part due to the active support of Trotsky, by the end of that decade the Stalinists were busy suppressing all manifestations of this interest. Similar opposition was encountered by the young left developing at the time within the psychoanalytical movement in the West, culminating in Reich's expulsion from the German Psychoanalytic Association in 1933—the same year that he was expelled from the German Communist Party, the KPD. As a result of these attempts to stifle the development of a new critical theory, and the subsequent annihilation of all independent intellectual and scientific life in Central Europe by fascism, the

---

psychology," for it was only by virtue of the postulation of such a level of human existence beyond immediate social control that it was possible to avoid the premature (and hence repressive) reconciliation of individual and society. Moreover, they argued, while Fromm was correct in asserting that Freudianism lacked an adequate comprehension of societal determinants, it was not true, as he also came to assert, that Freud's theory of the instincts constituted a mechanical division of the psyche into fixed, unalterable drives. On the contrary, Freud's use of instinct theory, far from hypostatizing biological drives, actually involved a highly dynamic derivation of psychic make-up from the interplay of pleasure-seeking and self-preservation motives—an interplay capable of almost infinite variation.

development of the Freudo-Marxist perspective, despite the immensely promising start made by theorists like Reich, Fromm, and Horkheimer, was forced to lead a largely subterranean existence among small groups of exiles and critical intellectuals outside the existing left parties. While important work still continued to be done, it attracted little attention and exercised little influence until a decade after the end of World War II, when with apparent suddenness, the links between psychoanalysis and Marxism were once again made explicit and discussion of the original Freudo-Marxist themes was taken up again, on the highest level in the work of Herbert Marcuse, as well as by such younger writers as Jürgen Habermas and Reimut Reiche. In the hands of this new generation of Freudo-Marxists, the initial attempt at sharpening the critical content of psychoanalytic concepts and elucidating their sociological character by integrating them within a new critical theory of society has been carried further, both through new efforts at a consistent synthesis and through the extension of the scope of this analysis to new problem areas (e.g., to the critical analysis of the functions of speech and language in the structure of the personality and its relation to the world, to a more critical understanding of the affective phenomena arising out of the relations of particular social groups to nature, to the formulation of psychoanalytically informed Marxist anthropology, etc.). Despite all obstacles, this project has been carried on up to the present and remains a living current of revolutionary thought. On the basis of the insights provided by the accumulated studies it has carried on regarding the interplay of social determinants and prevailing instinctual structures in the formation of character and consciousness, it has sought not only to construct a more global account of the totality of the economic, cultural, and psychological processes constituting the historical development of societies, but also to lay the foundations for a whole new critical theory of society.

Notes

1. Alexander Mitscherlich, *Society Without the Father* (New York, 1970), p. 10.
2. See Trent Schroyer's chapter entitled "The Idea of Emancipatory Critique" in his forthcoming *The Critique of Domination*, to be published by George Braziller in 1973. For somewhat different presentations of the position that there is an intrinsic "complementarity" between historical materialism and psychoanalysis as mutually dependent moments in an (as yet not fully articulated) dialectical anthropology, see also J.-P. Sartre, *Search for a Method* (New York, 1963); Edgar Morin, "L'homme revolutionné et l'homme revolutionnaire: l'homme marxien, l'homme freudien et la revolution du XXe siècle," *Socialisme ou Barbarie*, no. 39 (March–April 1965), pp. 1–15; Robert Kalidova, "Marx et Freud," *l'Homme et la Société*, no. 7 (January–February–March 1968), pp. 99–114 and no. 8 (April–May–June 1968), pp. 135–47.
3. Although approaches to this problematic can be discerned as early as 1909 in Ernst Bloch's writings on psychoanalysis, the most significant attempts at a synthesis of Marx and Freud date from the late 1920s, with the appearance of Siegfried Bernfeld's "Sozialismus und Psychoanalyse," *Der Klassenkampf*, no. 2 (1928), and Reich's "Dialectischer Materialismus und Psychoanalyse," *Unter dem Banner des Marxismus*, no. 3 (1929). In the latter work, in particular, it was argued that "just as Marxism was sociologically the expression of man *becoming conscious* of the laws of economics and the exploitation of a majority by a minority, so psychoanalysis is the expression of man *becoming conscious* of the social repression of sex." Only three years later, Horkheimer similarly inaugurated the Frankfort School's enduring concern with the problems of uniting historical materialism and psychoanalysis in his article "Ge-

schichte und Psychologie," *Zeitschrift für Sozialforschung*, vol. 1, no. 1 (1932).

4. Arnold Hauser, "The Psychological Approach: Psychoanalysis and Art," in his *The Philosophy of Art History* (Cleveland, 1963), p. 76.

5. See Boris Fraenkel, "Le freudo-marxisme," *l'Homme et la Société*, no. 11 (January–February–March 1969).

6. See Hauser, "The Psychological Approach," pp. 66–71, 77–83. Also see Igor Caruso, "Psychoanalysis and Society," *New Left Review*, no. 32 (July–August 1965), pp. 24–31.

7. Sigmund Freud, *Civilization and Its Discontents*, Strachey translation (New York, 1962), pp. 60–61. It is interesting to note the little-known fact that, at least according to Reich's own account, Freud wrote *Civilization and Its Discontents* largely in response to the increasingly radical direction taken by the development of Reich's thinking as revealed by his participation in the special monthly seminars held at Freud's home in 1929 and 1930. See Reich's *The Function of the Orgasm* (New York, 1961), pp. 165–68.

8. See Herbert Marcuse, "Critique of Neo-Freudian Revisionism," appendix to *Eros and Civilization: A Philosophical Inquiry into Freud* (New York, 1962), pp. 217–51; and T. W. Adorno, "Sociology and Psychology," *New Left Review*, no. 46 (November–December 1967) and no. 47 (January–February 1968).

9. Shulamith Firestone, *The Dialectic of Sex: The Case for Feminist Revolution* (New York, 1970), p. 70.

10. André Breton, "Prolegomena to a Third Surrealist Manifesto or Not," in André Breton, *Manifestoes of Surrealism* (Ann Arbor, 1969), p. 282.

11. Wilhelm Reich, "On Freud's Eightieth Birthday" (1936), in *Reich Speaks of Freud* (New York, 1967), p. 267.

12. A good account of the development of this psychoanalytic left is to be found in chapter 3 of Martin Jay's dissertation (see chapter 1, n. 25), entitled "The Integration of Psychoanalysis."

13. Erich Fromm, "Die Gesellschaftliche Bedingheit der psychoanalystischen Therapie," *Zeitschrift für Sozialforschung*, vol. 4, no. 3 (1935), p. 395.

14. Reich, "On Freud's Eightieth Birthday," p. 260.
15. Norman O. Brown, *Life Against Death: The Psychoanalytical Meaning of History* (Middletown, Conn., 1970), p. 124.
16. See Erich Fromm, "The Theory of Mother Right and Its Relevance for Social Psychology" (1934), in his *The Crisis of Psychoanalysis: Essays on Freud, Marx, and Social Psychology* (New York, 1970), pp. 84–109; and Wilhelm Reich, *The Invasion of Compulsory Sex-Morality* (New York, 1971).
17. See Bronislaw Malinowski, *The Sexual Life of Savages in Northwestern Melanesia* (London, 1930), and *Sex and Repression in Savage Society* (1927).
18. Reich, *The Function of the Orgasm*.
19. Wilhelm Reich, "Dialectical Materialism and Psychoanalysis," *Studies on the Left*, vol. 6, no. 4 (1966), p. 16.
20. Erich Fromm, "Uber Methode und Aufgabe einer analytischen Sozialpsychologie," *Zeitschrift für Sozialforschung*, vol. 1 (1932). I quote from the English translation of this essay in Fromm, *The Crisis of Psychoanalysis*, p. 134.
21. See particularly Reich's essay on "Roheim's Psychoanalysis of Primitive Cultures," included as an appendix to his *The Invasion of Compulsory Sex-Morality*, pp. 171–210.
22. Caruso, "Psychoanalysis and Society," p. 28, and Sartre, *Search for a Method*, pp. 60–62.
23. See Fromm, "Psychoanalytic Characterology and its Relevance for Social Psychology, in *The Crisis of Psychoanalysis*, esp. pp. 148–49; and Caruso, "Psychoanalysis and Society," pp. 27–28.
24. Letter from Louis Althusser to Ben Brewster of February 21, 1969, quoted in "Publisher's Note to 'Freud & Lacan,' " in Louis Althusser, *Lenin and Philosophy* (New York, 1972).
25. Friedrick Engels, Preface to the first edition of *Origin of the Family, Private Property and the State* (New York, 1942), p. 5.
26. Wilhelm Reich, *The Sexual Revolution* (New York, 1969), pp. 71–72.
27. Published in Paris in 1936. A summary of the various researches making up this study may be found in Martin Jay's dissertation, pp. 231–299.
28. Reich, *The Sexual Revolution*, p. 73.
29. Ibid., pp. 78–79.

30. Wilhelm Reich, *La lutte sexuelle des jeunes* (Paris, 1966), p. 124.
31. Fromm, "The Theory of Mother Right," p. 97.
32. Adorno, "Sociology and Psychology," Part I, pp. 75–76.
33. Max Horkheimer, "Authority and the Family." I quote from the translation published by Herder and Herder as part of the first volume of the English edition of his *Critical Theory* (New York, 1973), p. 128.
34. Ibid., p. 65.
35. Ibid, p. 58.
36. Ibid., p. 54.
37. Reich, *The Invasion of Compulsory Sex-Morality*, p. 166.
38. Fromm, "The Method and Function of Analytic Social Psychology," in *The Crisis of Psychoanalysis*, p. 133.
39. Fromm, "The Theory of Mother Right," p. 99.
40. Reich, "On Freud's Eightieth Birthday," p. 266.
41. Fromm, "The Method and Function of an Analytic Social Psychology," pp. 133–34.
42. A detailed historical introduction, along with the most important intellectual documents in this controversy between Marxists and Freudians, on the one hand, and those who sought a synthesis of the two perspectives and the institutional "Establishments" of both schools, on the other, is to be found in Hans Jörg Sankühler, ed., *Psychoanalyse und Marxismus: Dokumentation einer Kontroverse* (Frankfurt, 1970), pp. 7–45. See also, Constantin Sinelnikov, "Early 'Marxist' Critiques of Reich," *Telos*, no. 13 (Fall 1973), pp. 131–37.

3

Toward a New
Critical Theory

In the light of these developments leading toward the convergence of Marxism and psychoanalysis, we may now consider the actual contours and nature of the new critical theory which was arising from the interplay of specific studies and partial analyses of the social determinants and instinctual structures that made up the main thrust of the Freudo-Marxist endeavor. To be sure, the broad contours of this theory remained for a long time only implicit or, at best, were only partially and inadequately conceptualized in the work of the first two generations of Freudo-Marxists. Even today their aim of fully comprehending society as an interconnecting totality of economic, institutional, and psychological processes is far from being an actuality. Nevertheless, despite the continued presence of ambiguities, of divergent developments, of contradictory formulations, it is possible to discern in the diversity of points of view certain convergent themes and areas of concern which suggest the nature of the new theoretical synthesis immanent in this convergence.

We may discern, for example, a mutual point of departure for all those engaged in the Freudo-Marxist endeavor in their common recognition that between the two extreme poles in Marx's analysis—the socioeconomic structure of society and the ideological superstructures—lie a number of intermediate levels which have to be taken into account in both their "interrelatedness" and their specificity if an adequate comprehension of real forces "overdetermining" the movement of societies in history is to be achieved. This recognition of the specificity of various "superstructural" elements, and of the fact that they possess a reality of their own, is not simply a matter of repeating the admonition made by Engels late in his life against "overemphasizing the economic factor." Rather, it implies an entirely new extension of the dialectic to encompass cultural representations and the psychic make-up of individuals as factors which, instead of merely "reflecting" material constraints, are integral and defining aspects of a historical situation and can themselves act either to constrain the development of material processes or to anticipate new material possibilities in these situations.[1] Finally, inasmuch as this enterprise aspires toward the development of a unified theory of this complex interplay between the material life-processes underlying the development of specific modes of production and the historical transformations of human nature taking place within the framework of these transformations of social organization in the process of society's struggle to establish its collective mastery over nature, on the one hand, and the interaction of these factors conditioning the formation of this psychic make-up with the various cultural forces of the time, on the other, it also implies the necessity of replacing the exclusive emphasis placed by materialist analysis on the labor process as determinative of the totality of human existence with a less one-sided approach.[2] This approach sees the process by which the human species has historically constituted itself as finding expression not merely in the form of work, but also in historical action and creativity, in imagination and play, in language and communication. To be sure, this dichotomy between the material life-processes and culture should not itself be made into an ontological fact; it is not eternal but rather represents the form taken by the historical development of repressive civilization. In a truly rational society, work and culture might again be integrated. But since this integration remains a mere utopian hope under present conditions of capitalist irrationality, only such a two-sided approach appears capable of comprehending such phenomena as the persistence of social and cultural forms which are objectively anachronistic or, more generally, of restoring the intelligibility of events and social processes.

Hence, the relevance of psychoanalysis. Whereas Marxism can account for the development of socioeconomic structures in terms of its notion of the self-constitution of the human species in natural history as a process of self-production through labor, its model of productive activity is unable to give an equally adequate reconstruction of the formation of the various superstructural spheres—of the processes of self-formation, of power, and of communcation.[3] In contrast, psychoanalysis is able to provide a framework for the conceptualization of the origins of institutions and the role and function of power and ideology on the basis of an analysis of a structure that Marx did not fathom. The assimilation of the psychoanalytic critique revealed that the key to deciphering these complex processes lies in the recognition that underlying the relations of production and the socioeconomic organization of society are equally fundamental structures of affective relations and, hence, that societies must be understood simultaneously as functional totalities characterized by a particular social and technical division of labor and mode of exploitation and as affective totalities, whose driving elements are feelings and desires, fears and anxieties, fantasies and dreams, etc.

Marx was unable to grasp how such modalities of desire and inner compulsion, through which the libidinal and psycho-affective strivings of human beings are organized, underlie the organization of social and economic activity. This was because, as Habermas has pointed out,[4] Marx made the assumption that men distinguish themselves from animals simply by virtue of their development of a capacity to produce their means of subsistence: he saw man essentially as a tool-making animal. Freud, in contrast, because he started from the assumption that men distinguish themselves from animals when they succeed in inventing an agency of socialization for their biologically endangered offspring, subject to extended childhood dependency, uniquely grasped the affective dimensions missing in the Marxist analysis. More specifically, Freud, focusing not on the system of social labor but on the family, argued, as Habermas puts it, that "the human species elevated itself above animal conditions of existence by transcending the limits of animal society and being able to transform instinct-governed behavior into communicative action." [5] It follows that for Freud the key to understanding the natural basis of history lay in the analysis of "the physical organization specific to the human species under the category of surplus impulses and their canalization." [6] Man, instead of being defined exclusively as a tool-making animal, is seen even more primordially as the animal distinguishing itself from all other animals by its potential ability to control instinctual impulses and rechannel them toward other ends—that is, as "the drive-inhibited and at the same time fantasizing animal." [7]

From the psychoanalytic perspective, "the two-stage development of human sexuality, which is interrupted by a latency period owing to Oedipal repression, and the role of aggression in the establishment of the super-ego make man's basic problem not the organization of labor but the evolution of institutions that permanently solve the conflict between surplus impulses and the constraints of reality." [8] In keeping with this orientation, the principal emphasis is put upon "the destiny of the primary impulse potentials in the course of the growing child's interaction with an environment, determined by his family structure, on which he remains dependent during a long period of up-bringing." [9] Inasmuch as this process of repressive socialization—carried on, above all, by the family through the paternal authority's suppression, frustration, and redirection of the child's pleasure-seeking impulse—provides a "natural" basis for institutional authority as the collective form through which society organizes the further pursuit of substitute gratifications corresponding to the internal compulsions already established during primary socialization, and which, by associating these earliest impressions with later patterns of experience in which there is a larger element of conscious control, extends childhood dependency by transforming it into social domination, then it follows that there is a fundamental connection between the "ontogenetic" process by which the repressed individual has been created and the "phylogenetic" process by which repressive civilization has been produced. This connection, however, remains implicit in Freud's original formulation, due to the unhistorical character of certain of Freud's concepts.

Accordingly, the first task of a psychoanalytically informed critical theory is to elucidate how the " 'unhistorical' character of the Freudian concepts thus contains the elements of its opposite" and hence to derive "from Freud's theory [those] notions and propositions implied in it only in a reified form, in which historical processes appear as natural (biological) processes." [10] In opening up the question of how the psychic dynamism inherent in the human family might, in the fullness of time, produce the *antimony* between master and slave and the institution of the state, Freud "reaches down to the level where social and natural institutions are truly joined";[11] at the same time, as Marcuse has shown, his argument regarding the Oedipal origins and perpetuations of guilt only makes sense as a psychological moment within a larger sociological dynamic in which the instinctual processes of individual repression are anonymously generalized through their incorporation into a hierarchical social and economic division of labor. In other words, the logic of domination, which Freud locates in the instinctual processes, must also be understood as a historical process in which the psycho-affective complexes studied by psychoanalysis and the socioeconomic conflicts analyzed by Marxism constitute themselves, in their relation to the material life-processes by which society attempts to exert its organized mastery over nature, as distinct moments in a larger dialectic. Within this triadic dialectic of nature-man-culture (society) through which, according to Marcuse, domination has ruled the development of civilization, "the repressive transformation of the instincts becomes the biological constitution of the organism: history rules even in the instinctual structure; culture becomes nature as soon as the individual learns to affirm and to reproduce the reality principle from within himself, through his instincts." [12] As a result, the individual becomes, *"in his very nature*, the subject-object of socially useful labor, of the domination of men and nature." [13] For Marcuse, "as soon as civilized society establishes itself, the repressive transformation of the instincts becomes the psychological basis of a *threefold domination:* first, domination over oneself, over one's own nature, over the sensual drives that want only pleasure and gratification; second, domination of the labor achieved by such disciplined and controlled individuals; and third, domination of outward nature, science and technology." [14]

Here, then, "is the psychoanalytic key to a social theory that converges in a surprising way with Marx's reconstruction of the history of the [human] species, while in another regard advancing specifically new perspectives." [15] Such a psychoanalytic anthropology, if consistently developed, would view "civilization" in the same way Marx comprehends society, "as the means by which the human species elevates itself above animal conditions of existence" and as "a system of self-preservation that serves two functions in particular: self-assertion against nature and the organization of men's interrelations." [16] "Like Marx, though in different terms," this perspective would distinguish forces of production—that is, the level of technical control achieved by society over natural processes—from relations of production. Developing the anthropological implications of Freud's thought thus involves rendering the psychoanalytic perspective capable of generating a materialist conception of history.

Marcuse in particular has attempted to reformulate the Marxian dialectic of needs-labor-fulfillment (or consumption) in the process of society's progressive domination over nature, which is properly the province of political economy, in its relation to the more psychosociological dialectic of needs-work-desire by which the instinctual or natural needs that relate men to nature are transformed into the accomplished human desires that relate men to other men within a humanized social world that is quite distinct from the natural world. He has put forward two original concepts: first, the *performance principle*, the prevailing historical form of the reality principle through which this socialization of instinctual energies into social labor in the interests of societal self-preservation takes place; second, *surplus repression*, the restrictions which arise out of this process over and above the "basic repression" necessary for societal self-preservation, and which serve instead to reproduce social domination. For Marcuse, it is through the operation of the performance or productivity principle, which has hitherto characterized the whole historical existence of humanity and within which labor has constituted a personal act of self-preservation that takes up practically the whole of an individual's life-span, that the natural tendency toward the pursuit of pleasure in the form of immediate gratification has been "suspended" and that, in this way, the "somatic-psychic" basis for the development of human mastery over nature has been created. Marcuse emphasizes how the dialectic of civilization has unfolded historically under the rule of this principle in terms of the development of the self in its struggle against nature in general, against other people in particular, and against its own impulses, on the one hand, and the development of the organization of labor through this process, on the other. He suggests the following steps:

First, repressive modifications of sexuality make the organism free to be used as an instrument of unpleasurable but socially useful labor. *Second*, if this labor is a life-long chief occupation—that is, [if it] has become the universal means of life—then the original direction of the instincts is so distorted that the content of life is no longer gratification, but rather working toward it. *Third*, in this way, civilization reproduces itself on an increasingly extended scale. The energy won from sexuality and sublimated constantly increases the psychic "investment fund" for the increasing productivity of labor (technical progress). *Fourth*, increasing productivity of labor increases the possibility of enjoyment and thus the potential reversal of the socially compelled relationship between labor and enjoyment, labor time and free time. But the domination reproduced in the existing relationships also reproduces subordination on an increasing scale: the goods produced for enjoyment remain commodities, the enjoyment of which presupposes further labor within existing relationships. Gratification remains a by-product of ungratifying labor. Increasing productivity itself becomes the necessity which it was to eliminate. Thus, *fifth*, the sacrifices that socialized individuals have imposed on themselves since the fall of the primal father become increasingly more irrational, the more obviously reason has fulfilled its purpose and eliminated the original state of need. And the guilt which the sacrifices were to expiate through the deification and internalization of the father (religion and morality) remain unexpiated, because with the reestablishment of patriarchal authority, although in the form of rational universality, the (suppressed) wish for its annihilation remains alive.[17]

It is in regard to this process—the achievement of the growing domination of nature through the growing internalization of repression—that Marcuse introduces the notion of *surplus repression* in order to account for the manner in which the reality principle (in this case, the performance principle) has at every point in the historical development of civilization also found embodiment in a specific system of societal institutions and relations, of laws and values, which affect the content of the reality principle itself. In this way, "the processes that create the ego and the superego also shape and perpetuate specific societal institutions and relations," [18] which are perpetuated by the need dispositions of the individuals who exhibit these traits as represented by the reality principle in a particular epoch. Thus the reality principle becomes materialized in a system of institutions, and "the individual, growing up within such a system, learns the requirements of the reality principle as those of law and order, and transmits them to the next generation." [19] It follows that the evolution of the reality principle as performance principle has taken various historical forms in relation to the simultaneous evolution of the various modes of domination (of man and nature). The industrial performance principle under classical capitalism, for example, is from the psychoanalytic point of view an anal performance principle which manifests itself in the generalization of a social personality broadly resembling what Freud called the "anal-obsessive type." [20] As a result of the direction given to character and consciousness, to needs and desires, by the reworking of instinctual impulses under the rule of this anal-obsessive personality, the system of socioeconomic domination complemented the external forces at its disposal by a powerful form of inner compulsion serving not only to focus the psychic energies of individuals on the attainment of rational mastery over nature, but also, by wiping out the recollection of all previous states of relatively greater satisfaction of needs (e.g., the former identity of production and consumption in stationary economies), to inspire a compulsive identification by individuals with the system's goals. As capitalism succeeded in imposing these anal-obsessive types on individuals, it was able to guarantee that through their compulsive activity they would in turn reproduce the forms of private economic power on which the system was based, even in the face of objective disruptions of economic reproduction by periodic crises.[21]

In short, by adding the essential "internal inputs" necessary to keep this process going to the "external inputs" provided by the technical innovation and rationalization of economic life by which the capitalist mode of production has continually been revolutionized—that is, by creating "a social personality capable of guiding the process while at the same time remaining completely subordinate to it" [22]—the anal performance principle was an essential component in the adaptation of individuals to the priorities of capital accumulation under the auspices of private economic production for profit during the first industrial age.

Naturally, an industrial performance principle in a later stage of industrialization, in a society oriented toward individual consumption instead of profit, or in a system regulated by central planning instead of a market, would take different forms. Not only do these differences in socio-economic organization affect the very content of the reality principle embodied within particular systems of societal institutions as it expresses itself through the required repression modification of instincts, but also, in addition to the considerable degree and scope of repressive control over the instincts engendered by any form of the reality principle, "the specific historical institutions of the reality principle and the specific interests of domination [also] introduce *additional* controls over and above those indispensable for civilized human association." [23] It is these additional controls, arising from the specific institutions of domination, that Marcuse denotes as surplus repression:

> For example, the modifications and deflections of instinctual energy necessitated by the perpetuation of the monogamic-patriarchal family, or by a hierarchical division of labor, or by public control over the individual's private existence are instances of surplus-repression pertaining to the institutions of a *particular* reality principle. They are added to the basic (phylogenetic) restrictions of the instincts which mark the development of man from the human animal to the *animal sapiens*.[24]

Marcuse's analysis clearly represents a giant step forward in assimilating psychoanalysis into Marxism within a new critical theory of society. At the same time, this analysis reveals that the extent to which the processes through which the logic of domination has unfolded within the development of civilization cannot be reconstructed solely in terms of the necessary repression required for self-preservation in the face of material scarcity, but also requires us to take account of the evolution of specific systems of institutions and modes of domination of a relatively stable character. It suggests the necessity of going beyond Marcuse's own reconstruction of this historical development in terms of a simple dialectic within which the ontogenetic processes of the self-formation of the repressed individual are linked to the phylogenetic processes giving rise to the repressive civilization as a whole exclusively through the mediation of the organization of labor. Although Marcuse recognizes the sociocultural sphere as a distinct subsystem created through the emergence of a process of organization and communicative action within a

wider societal system, he at the same time adopts an overly
naturalistic conception of the dynamics of the instincts in
their confrontations with reality as the prime mover of this
process of human self-constitution.

While specifying the necessity of an organizing principle
(the primal father) for this development, Marcuse fails to
recognize that the actual significance of such a principle is
not as a statement about history or reality as such, but rather
consists of its *symbolic* function.[25] In this regard, it should be
clear, as John O'Neill puts it, that

> the transformation of the mother-child bond into the order of
> the social division of labor, in turn variously subject to the
> frameworks of kinship and rational legal sanctions, is possible
> precisely because of the largely *symbolic* nature of human
> embodiment and reproduction—the traumas of union and
> separation [for example] are repeated in the symbolic lan-
> guages of the psychic and political orders, and thereby furnish
> the fundamental categories of alienation, exchange, and
> communion.[26]

Thus, on the human level we never encounter any needs that
have not first been "interpreted linguistically and symbolically affixed to specific forms of activity and which, therefore,
unlike the unreconstructed impulse potentials rooted in the
natural or biological sphere," have become knowable precisely insofar as "they define the situation of the conflict
through which the species has been struggling" [27]—that is,
insofar as they take on the culturally conditioned forms of
work, language, and power, through which this conflict
manifests itself. It follows that culture cannot be seen as
arising directly out of instinctual drives or out of conflicts
between them, but only through the unique action of a
consciousness characterized by its ability to produce symbolic representations. It is necessary to recognize that the
mediations between a human group or a society and nature

are characterized by a dualistic organization of these relations. The first are, in effect, economic and are organized
according to causal determinations susceptible to an over-
determined effect; the second are symbolic and are organized
according to systems of signs and their own internal relations.
It is only by virtue of this second set of relations that the
processes of self-formation through which the human species
secures its existence in systems of social labor and institutions
can, on the level of ordinary-language communication, re-
consolidate the consciousness of the individual relative to the
norms of the group and form the ego identities appropriate
to each particular stage of individuation through the conflict
between instinctual aims and social constraints.

Thus Habermas, as against Marcuse's tendency to subsume
the problems of symbolically mediated interaction within a
dialectics of labor, has emphasized the irreducibility of the
two spheres.[28] Whereas the former involves the self-production of the human species through the transformation of
surplus instinctual energy into social labor, the latter process,
through which institutions and culture take form, only arises
on the basis of the accomplished transformation of instinctual needs into those human desires which have as their sole
referent a social not a biological context, and which therefore develop through a dynamic which is discontinuous with
the dynamic of the instincts. While the notion of surplus
repression may be essential in order to explain the origin of
the sociocultural sphere as a system of symbolically mediated
interactions, it is not in and of itself sufficient for a
reconstruction of the dialectic of institutions (i.e., of "insti-
tuted" structures and "instituting" practices) underlying the
subsequent development and transformation of this sphere
through which the conflicts between surplus impulse potentials and the conditions of collective self-preservation find
their actual expression in social practice. What is required is
rather a broader framework for the reconstruction of the

self-formation of the human species, capable of incorporating the Marcusean insights within a larger totalization which encompasses the specificity of this sociocultural sphere. Such an analysis would have to draw particularly on the work of Habermas (or, from a somewhat different perspective, Jacques Lacan),[29] which, without denying the biological basis of the instincts, nevertheless comprehends the drives as they present themselves through the unconscious—not on the basis of a vague analogy to organic mechanisms, but rather in terms of their conflictual manifestations, first of all as forms of linguistic failure, of systematically distorted communication (e.g., dreams, so-called Freudian slips, neurotic symptoms, etc.).

From this perspective, neurotic and psychotic symptoms are revealed as forms of distorted or repressive communication which the sufferer normally adopts in response to a childhood inability to resolve some libidinal conflict and to the consequent need for the child, and in turn the adult, to exclude the object of this conflict from public communication. Out of this process of desymbolization and symptom formation which results from the individual's adoption of a private language and use of "deviant linguistic rules" arise all the typical forms of psychosis and neurosis, of repetition compulsion, and, finally, the very disjunctions between ego, superego, and id as spheres corresponding to different levels of communication.[30] This multi-layered structure of repressive communication, as Claus Mueller has shown, is not simply internal to the individual, but is also determinant of the individual's relation to society.

> On the individual level, any incongruence between inner and outer language, between privatized and externalized meaning, any split in the symbols used, any incapacity to integrate symbolically one's biographic experience will not only result in a distorted monologue with oneself but also in distorted communication with others. This distortion constitutes the

repressive nature of the communication. The common characteristic of repressive communication is that the internalized language system permits neither the articulation of subjectively experienced needs beyond the emotive level nor the realization of maximum individuation. . . . On the psychic level, the language used represses parts of one's symbolic biography and inhibits the attainment of consciousness. On the class level, the language used results in an incapacity to locate oneself in history and society.[31]

Since these forms of communicative behavior rest not only on language but also on work and on power relations, it follows that inasmuch as the typification schemes of language come to constitute the most fundamental rules of everyday life, they find their social expression in the formation of institutions. In this regard it is clear that language, as the fundamental means of sustaining institutions—which, in fact, are themselves a sort of language, just as language itself is an institution—provides a crucial and hitherto missing link in our analysis of the relationship between the "ontogenetic" and "phylogenetic" spheres. Habermas has reformulated this relationship as involving not only the means by which the human species ensures its survival through the creation of systems of social labor and coercive self-assertion, but also as involving the creation of relatively stable forms of traditionally mediated common life in colloquial linguistic communication. What characterizes institutions, for Habermas, is what characterizes their similarity to pathological forms: they represent devices for the exchange of acute external force for the permanent internal compulsions of distorted and self-limited communication which, like neurotic solutions at the individual level, function as collective solutions to the problem of self-preservation—"like the repetition compulsion from within, institutional compulsion from without brings about a relatively rigid reproduction of relatively uniform behavior that is removed from criticism."[32] Like individual acts of repression, the collective internalizations of compulsion which have given rise to both historic institutions and cultural traditions are seen as arising under conditions of material scarcity as a result of the necessary suppression of surplus instinctual impulses as the pursuit of these drives comes into conflict with the constraints of reality and must be diverted into substitute channels of gratification.

This "suggests a comparison of the world-historical process of social organization with the socialization process of the individual." [33] Just as neurosis and psychosis are the individual's mode of existence in response to biological and social alienations, the forms of the dominant culture and the institutional apparatus of a society are based on the substitution of hidden, internal compulsions for external restraints in such a way as to prohibit and suppress the pursuit of needs outside of culturally sanctioned channels. "Motivation and institutional structure," in Philip Slater's words, "are thus twinned, like the hedgehog and his wife in the folktale." [34] Like technology, they constitute materializations of the fantasies of past generations, inflicted on the present in the form of compulsory norms which are in turn enforced through circular processes of compulsion, operating both to suppress the capacity of the individual to interpret his or her need dispositions, and to prohibit, to suppress and sanction interpreted needs so as to create a symbolic system of enforced substitute gratifications whose character becomes fixed, opaque, and without reciprocity. In this way, the institutional framework of a class society comes to constitute a self-reproducing system of power which is imposed on all its members and which serves to censor and channel surplus instinctual impulses and energies toward ends which are predefined as "legitimate."

Once the natural basis of the human species is seen as essentially determined by the rechanneling of surplus impulses and by extended childhood dependency, and once the origin of institutions is comprehended on this basis, it follows that the spheres of culture and of the "superstructures" take on a different and more substantial role than they do in the conventional Marxist analysis of the institutional framework as simply an ordering of interests that are immediately functions of the system of social labor according to the relations of social rewards and imposed obligations that are, in turn, rooted in force and distorted according to class structure. Although these cultural forms and institutionalized power relations are, in the last analysis, dependent on the objective possibilities posed by the development of the productive forces, they are nonetheless not directly reducible to the organization of these forces. While it is true that the institutional framework of the system of social labor serves the functional needs of the system by organizing both the cooperation of labor in production and the distribution of goods in the sphere of consumption, at the same time it must also serve to stabilize institutionally the social and technical division of labor which arises out of this process. "For, under the pressure of reality, not all interpreted needs find gratification, and socially transcendent motives of action cannot all be defended against with consciousness, but only with the aid of affective forces." [35] To the extent that the principle of social regulation, in depriving these impulses of direct, spontaneous satisfaction, finds compensatory satisfaction elsewhere, it creates a *new reality*, a "spiritual" or "imaginary" reality forming an ideal sphere for impulse satisfaction —that is, a sphere of compensations. There thus arises a secondary level of human existence which is both "ideology" and "structure" and which gives institutions their singular character, over and above the socioeconomic determinants of their forms, as products of symbolism and as contexts for continual symbolization.[36] The dynamics of symbolically mediated interaction, while always interlocked with the dynamics of self-production through labor, are therefore an irreducible mechanism. Cultural tradition emerges out of this process of symbol formation as the sum of those specific forms and projections which have arisen "as sublimations that represent suspended gratifications and guarantee publicly sanctioned compensations for the necessary cultural renunciation." [37] Since, unlike individual fantasies, "they are not private, but instead, on the level of public communication itself, lead a split-off existence that is removed from criticism, they are elaborated into interpretations of the world and taken into service as rationalizations of authority." [38]

These symbols, fantasies, and images, materialized in institutions and preserved in cultural tradition, are not static but undergo continual transformation as change in society's mental apparatus interacts with the historical processes tending to transform the physical world. The basic function of the cultural sphere, as an organized symbolic network of substitute gratifications, remains the same, but the ways it expresses this function undergo profound transformation. Within primitive societies, for example, culture in general tends to be encompassed almost exclusively within the framework of religious symbolism. For the members of such societies, "this symbolism, in effect, is total, both cosmological and anthropological: it seeks to govern man's relation to the universe, men's relations to each other, and the immanent equilibrium of man himself as a part of the world and a member of society." [39] In its function of culturalizing the great events of natural origin, the order of religious symbolism within pre-industrial societies tends to be linked to the whole of social practices. By virtue of their universality, these religious symbols and collective fantasies have an essential advantage over individual fantasies and dreams, for they are perceived by the conscious mind as if they were real; as Fromm puts it, "an illusion shared by everyone becomes a reality." [40] Moreover, inasmuch as it is first and foremost through religion that the behavior of the natural (i.e., instinctual) being becomes transformed into the normalized and socialized behavior of man as a *cultural* being, not only does religious symbolism sanctify life, procreation, and death, but it also provides the sociocultural foundation for all those pressures and repressions imposed on individuals by society and ultimately internalized by them. It is therefore within the religious sphere that there first appears the substitutional character generally typical of cultural symbolism in its subsequent secular forms: "Insofar as society does not permit real satisfactions, [these] fantasy satisfactions serve as a substitute and become a powerful support of social stability." [41] Toward this fundamental purpose of rationalizing repression and domination, not only religious world views and ritual, but also artistic products, values, and moral codes, etc., have all been constructed from the projected contents of wish-fantasies expressing impulses censored in varying degrees and turned outward toward socially defined substitute channels—a development strengthened and accelerated by the customary activities of civilization's ruling minorities and their ideologists who, in order to guide the aggressive drives of the masses into socially harmless channels, have the task of suggesting ever new forms of symbolic satisfaction to them. The sacrifice and repression of the real and immediate life of the masses finds in the symbolic order its inverted image in a system of mythical rewards and compensations for real deprivations.

To be sure, the hedonistic ideologies of the rising bourgeoisie appeared to assert the claims of human happiness and real gratification against the old religious ideals of suffering, renunciation, and sacrifice; but in practice they only opposed the old forms of repression in order to invent new, more rational, but more pervasive ones. Protestantism seems to mark a whole new stage in the complicated process of civilizational development by which compulsion has been progressively internalized in the form of inner constraints. Although the existence of such forms of internal compulsion did not originate with Protestantism, or with the rise of capitalism for that matter, but is found throughout previous historical periods, the development of Protestantism in connection with the capitalist mode of production nonetheless remains exceptional in that it involved the creation of a "performance principle" so firmly anchored in the mental structure of the individual that it no longer needed to be reimposed continually from without, but operated to generate compulsion from within in such a way as to reproduce itself internally.

In this regard, Protestantism can be seen as responding to the insufficiencies of medieval Catholicism with respect to the imperatives of the new bourgeoisie. "Far more astute and more rational than Roman Catholicism," remarks Henri Lefebvre, "[it] performed the repressive function of religion with greater subtlety; God and reason were the portion of each individual, everyone was his own mentor, responsible for the repression of his desires, the control of his instincts; the result was asceticism without an ascetic dogma, without anyone enforcing asceticism; the whipping boy and scapegoat being sexuality." [42] Protestantism came to provide the images and language that capitalism unobtrusively adopted: "[As] intention replaced ritual and faith supplanted works, this religion furthered the generalization of industry and trade that appropriated its values by appearing to respect them (conscience, faith, personal contact with God)." [43] Along the same lines, Marcuse has shown in his early essays how these changes resulting from further social and economic development not only resulted in the transformation of religion from its more primitive and magical forms into more complicated and rationalized ones, but also how culture in general became more differentiated and how side by side with the development of religion came all the more sophisticated developments of high culture—poetry, art, philosophy—as expressions of all the values which the new bourgeois society denied in the sphere of everyday life. According to Marcuse, this "affirmative culture," as he called the sublimated bourgeois culture with its anti-sexual, patricentric morality and its condemnation of hedonism and happiness in general in favor of an abstract "higher virtue," provided a necessary spiritual counterpart to Reich's repressive triangle of patriarchy, monogamy, and sexual repression. Within such an affirmative culture, happiness and the spirit, having been segregated from material life, are only then affirmed in a sublimated, hypostatized form as the purely spiritual realm called *Kulchur*. More specifically, "by affirmative culture is meant that culture of the bourgeois epoch which led in the course of its own development to the segregation from civilization of the mental and spiritual world as an independent realm of value that is also considered superior to civilization." [44] The most decisive characteristic of this culture is seen by Marcuse as "the assertion of a universally obligatory, eternally better, and more valuable world that must be unconditionally affirmed: a world essentially different from the factual world of the daily struggle for existence, yet realizable by every individual for himself 'from within' without any transformation of the state of fact."

The repressive functions of these claims made by the "inner world" of spiritual values upon the individual were reflected, first of all, in the replacement of happiness or "goodness" as a goal of life with a notion of duty and discipline, especially as regards economic activity, as the highest form of ethical self-regulation. Closely associated with the new attitudes toward work and property was the increasing dissociation of sexual pleasure from the bourgeois conception of love. Sexual love was stripped of its spontaneous character in conformity with the demands of bourgeois economic activity and was reduced to a mere matter of duty and habit; its principal function became that of maintaining an appropriate physical and spiritual context for the reproduction of the economic apparatus during a period of the individual accumulation of capital. This devaluation of sexuality corresponded, as Fromm has noted, to the reification of all human relationships within bourgeois society: "Along with this reification, an indifference to the fate of one's fellow man characterized relationships within the bourgeois world; there was no trace of individual responsibility for the lot of others, no hint of love for one's fellowmen as such without any conditions being attached." [45] At the same time as it attempts to forestall the revolutionary potential implicit in the release of sexuality by imposing a puritanical sexual morality on society, affirmative culture also functions to create alternative channels for the dammed-up libidinal energies thus created in the form of a network of substitute gratifications, from religion, to sports, to popular entertainment. Lastly, in terms of the structures of communicative action, we may describe such a society and culture as characterized by a sharp disjuncture between public and private language—that is, between the expressions of official symbols and predefinitions emanating from the institutions of class power and the expressions of individualized need and private meanings arising out of the everyday life of individuals.*

---

* "An individual may respond to this situation with what H. Arendt calls privatization of meaning. As the sociopolitical reality is mystified by the officially espoused paradigms, the individual withdraws from the public and ceases to interact symbolically, through language, in the political realm. Possible communication about politics becomes repressive as relevant information and adequate concepts and paradigms that are necessary for the understanding of politics are excluded from the public language. This exclusion is functional for the given political system since the available predefinitions support the mode of domination in that they

In all these ways, the affirmative culture provides the basis for a stabilization of class society and the reinforcement of class privilege by a process of incessant repression and evasion, compulsion, and adaptation, which diffuses the pressures and repressions arising out of socioeconomic relations throughout all the levels and spheres of experience making up everyday life: sexual and emotional experience, private and family life, childhood, adolescence, and maturity, etc.—in short, all those realms that would seem on the face of it to lie outside the socioeconomic mechanisms of repression by virtue of their "spontaneous" and "natural" character. Through its success in modifying the conditions of repression, its methods, means, and foundations, and by means of skillful compulsion aimed at directing adaptation into the channels of private experience and portraying freedom as something purely spiritual and ideal, such a cultural constellation increasingly replaces overt compulsion with forms of persuasion and self-compulsion that perfectly complement material oppression and supplement the repressive function of the central power in enforcing sanctions and taboos by increasingly entrusting its duties to intimate groups, to the family, to the father, and to the individual conscience. Henri Lefebvre has defined such a society—a society in which the apparent decline of the more brutal and violent forms in which compulsion had been exercised since ancient times have been superseded by more subtle yet incomparably more pervasive forms of terror which operate so as to create a convergence between compulsion and the illusion of freedom—as an "over-repressive" society:

> We may define an over-repressive society as one that, in order to avoid overt conflicts, adopts a language and an attitude

---

reduce the reflective potential implicit in the semantic and syntactic dimensions of ordinary language. A restriction of the semantic fields accomplished by removing from the public consciousness categories and associations related to key symbols serves to stabilize predefinitions." [46]

dissociated from conflicts, one that deadens or even annuls opposition; its outcome and materialization would be a certain type of (liberal) democracy where compulsions are neither perceived nor experienced as such; either they are recognized and justified, or they are explained away as the necessary conditions of (inner) freedom. Such a society holds violence in reserve and only makes use of it in emergencies; it relies more on the self-repression inherent in organized everyday life; re-repression becomes redundant in proportion to the performance of its duties by (individual or collective) *self-repression*. A society can proclaim that the Kingdom of Freedom is at hand when compulsion passes for spontaneity and *adaptation* no longer exists either in word or concept.[47]

In the light of this perspective regarding the dual determination of the self-constitution of the human species as arising out of the historical configurations of instrumental and symbolic interaction systems, it becomes possible to recognize the extent to which the constraints placed on the development of the forces of production by capitalist social relations have only been sustained by the development in turn of constraints on communicative interaction, and to shed new light on the nature of the possibilities arising out of this dialectic of the movement from nature to man to culture for the elaboration of analyses leading from the self-reflection on alienated conditions of existence through revolutionary practice to unalienated freedom. By thus reconstructing the manner in which our present-day society and civilization has arisen through the internalized subordination of individuals to the constraints of the need for collective self-preservation, and the external subordination of the great mass of individuals to the interests of the ruling groups, the new critical theory not only exposes the extent to which all hitherto existing culture has been organized in the interests of domination, but also reveals new sources of resistance to these forms of domination, and new conflicts between the claims of human desire and the renunciations hitherto imposed on these claims. Inasmuch as the logic of the new critical theory clearly implies that this basic conflict with the constraints of reality is defined by the conditions of material labor and economic scarcity, then the renunciations it imposes must likewise be a historically variable factor. Thus, for the individual the constraints represented by the reality principle and encountered by her/him in the social framework of institutionalized power appear as an immovable reality, as an insurmountable barrier to the realization of desires incompatible with its sanctions, which consequently can only find expression as fantasies and are shunted onto the path of substitute gratification; but for human society as a whole these boundaries are in fact movable. As Habermas has put it, inasmuch as "the degree of socially necessary repression can be measured by the variable extent of the power of technical control over natural processes," it follows that "with the development of technology, the institutional framework, which regulates the distribution of obligations and rewards and stabilizes a power structure that maintains cultural renunciation, can be loosened." [48]

The very process by which the system of institutionalized power maintains general repressions and imposes renunciations on society is therefore contradictory, in that this self-denial, which throughout previous centuries had been necessary to ensure the development of civilization under conditions of material scarcity, leads to a redirection of instinctual energies into social labor on such a scale as to result in the achievement of a level of technological development which makes such repressions in the future unnecessary for the continual reproduction of human civilization. The massive accumulation of capital made possible by this work discipline and self-denial has culminated in the development, in recent decades, of an automated and cybernetic technology which has finally brought to a close that long period, constituting the whole of human history up to now, in which the inevitability of scarcity and of endless toil for most women and men as the price of survival constituted the central fact of human existence. Thus, "what distinguishes our time from all earlier epochs is that by now in the advanced capitalist countries, the mechanism of repression has accomplished its historical mission." [49] Civilization now possesses emancipatory possibilities beyond the repressiveness of an affirmative culture justified by scarcity and the cultural elitism Freud and his orthodox followers saw as an objective necessity for civilized life. The old repressive culture, albeit at a terrible price, has produced the quantitative means for a qualitative change in human life and culture. Under these circumstances, as "technical progress opens up the possibility of reducing socially necessary repression below the level of institutionally demanded repression," [50] elements of cultural traditions which previously had only a "projective" content as substitute gratifications serving to stabilize existing institutions, can increasingly become subversive forces as men and women seek to actualize these collective fantasies by constructing new, alternative forms of social organization. The major illusions of humanity—the hopes and desires relegated to the purely "spiritual" realm during the epoch of scarcity—are not simply forms of false consciousness; they also harbor utopian dreams which, as this era recedes, might find expression in the demand that they be transposed from the sphere of *virtual* gratification into that of *real* gratification (for instance, in the fusion of the classical opposites of affirmative culture, of "sensuousness and reason, happiness and freedom," within a free society for all). In this way, the repressed utopian content of culture would "be freed from its fusion with the delusory, ideological components of culture that have been fashioned into legitimations of authority and be converted into a critique of power structures that have become historically obsolete." [51]

It is in this context that we may approach the question of the place of the class struggle, for whereas with the extension of the objective possibilities for liberation as a result of the development of the productive forces virtually everyone in a sense has an interest in the abolition of historically anachronistic forms of repression, at the same time the system of institutionalized power manufactures not only general repressions which victimize all members of society alike, but also *class specific* privations and denials which are imposed on the structure of general ones as a result of the domination of a specific ruling class. Inasmuch as the traditions and substitute gratifications that legitimate institutional authority must "also compensate the mass of the population for those specific renunciations that go beyond the general privations," [52] it is these oppressed masses in whom the fragility and declining integrative capacity of the prevailing legitimations first manifest themselves. It is also they who first discover the suppressed utopian content of culture and critically turn it against the established order. To be sure, just as these oppressed masses are not all victimized by class civilization to an equal extent and are affected in different ways by this victimization, so also does the process by which enlightenment and self-liberation come to correspond to the conscious interests of the great mass of humanity take place with an extreme unevenness. This increasing interest in self-emancipation arises first in those particular sectors of the proletariat which experience most sharply the restrictions on the satisfactions necessary for the expanded satisfactions available to the ruling groups and/or which have for one reason or another a less stable psychic make-up and hence a less highly developed internalization of class domination. Further, the possibility for such a coming-to-consciousness, which arises when society's growing mastery over nature makes existing legitimations less credible, only becomes an actuality for one or another sector of the proletariat through the mediating structures of a culture whose different elements develop in an equally uneven way, and which at any point may act either to sharpen or obscure the objective contradictions.

Within this complex interplay of cultural, characterological, and institutional development which mediates between objective social and economic developments and the subjective responses of individuals, groups, and classes to these developments, each group or individual only succeeds in actively responding, rather than passively adapting, inasmuch as he or she succeeds in transcending from the start and at every point all the constraints placed on this consciousness and action by an institutionalization of power relations which, although it arose out of scarcity and was necessary for the societal conquest of scarcity, has also, in the process of expanding society's domination over nature, served to expand the powers available for the domination of this society's members, concentrated in the hands of the ruling groups and available to them as means of prolonging this domination despite its obsolescence. As a consequence, there is no certainty that emancipation will follow from technological development tending to burst the confines of existing institutions and hence mobilizing the majority of those subordinate to these constraints into oppositional struggle. Instead, there is only a horizon of possibilities and opportunities for individuals and classes who have overcome the constraints of institutional and cultural legitimations to pose the question of emancipation and assert their claims in a struggle whose outcome remains open. Inasmuch as such a massive subjective rupture with existing forms of domination does not take place, the utopian potentialities represented by the development of the productive forces will not only go unrealized (and unrecognized) but will be converted to the interests of domination. As Habermas has remarked, any attempt to provide a rational justification for cultural prescriptions is undertaken with the understanding that an experiment is being carried out that may *fail*.

Notes

1. See Norman Birnbaum, "The Crisis in Marxist Sociology," in H. P. Dreitzel, ed., *Recent Sociology No. 1: The Social Basis of Politics* (New York, 1965), pp. 29–31.

2. See Martin Jay, "The Frankfurt School's Critique of Marxist Humanism," *Social Research*, vol. 39, no. 2 (Summer 1972); Trent Schroyer, "The Dialectical Foundations of Critical Theory," *Telos*, no. 12 (Summer 1972), pp. 93–114.

3. See Jürgen Habermas, "Knowledge and Human Interests: A General Perspective," in his *Knowledge and Human Interests* (Boston, 1971), pp. 301–17, and "Technology and Science as 'Ideology,' " in his *Toward a Rational Society* (Boston, 1970).

4. See Habermas, "Psychoanalysis and Social Theory," in *Knowledge and Human Interests*, pp. 281–82.

5. Ibid., p. 282.

6. Ibid.

7. Ibid., pp. 282–83.

8. Ibid., p. 283.

9. Ibid.

10. Marcuse, *Eros and Civilization*, p. 32.

11. Norman O. Brown, *Life Against Death*, p. 125.

12. Herbert Marcuse, "Freedom and Freud's Theory of Instincts," in *Five Lectures* (Boston, 1970), p. 11.

13. Ibid., p. 11.

14. Ibid., p. 12.

15. Habermas, "Psychoanalysis and Social Theory," p. 276.

16. Ibid., pp. 276–77.

17. Marcuse, "Freedom and Freud's Theory of Instincts," pp. 21–22.

18. Marcuse, *Eros and Civilization*, p. 180.

19. Ibid., p. 15.
20. See Fromm, "Psychoanalytic Characterology and its Relevance for Social Psychology," in *The Crisis of Psychoanalysis*, pp. 154–55. Fromm describes this anal-obsessive type as exhibiting the following traits: (1) the restriction of the role of pleasure as an end in itself (particularly sexual pleasure); (2) the retreat from love with the emphasis instead on collecting, possessing, and saving as ends in themselves; (3) the ascription of the highest value to the fulfillment of one's duty; (4) the compulsive pursuit of "orderliness" and the exclusion of compassion for one's fellow man.
21. See Reimut Reiche, *Sexuality and Class Struggle*, pp. 37–40.
22. Ibid., p. 37.
23. Marcuse, *Eros and Civilization*, p. 34.
24. Ibid., pp. 34–35.
25. See Anthony Wilden, "Marcuse and the Freudian Model: Energy Information and *Phantasie*," *Salmagundi* (Winter 1969), especially pp. 216–22.
26. John O'Neill, "On Body Politics," in H. P. Dreitzel, ed., *Recent Sociology No. 4: Family, Marriage, and the Struggle of the Sexes* (New York, 1972), p. 254.
27. Habermas, "Psychoanalysis and Social Theory," p. 286.
28. See Habermas, "Technology and Science as 'Ideology,'" in *Toward a Rational Society*, as well as Jeremy Schapiro's "From Marcuse to Habermas," in *Continuum*, vol. 8, no. 1 (Spring–Summer 1970), pp. 65–76.
29. On Lacan see the essay by Althusser, "Freud and Lacan," in *Lenin and Philosophy*, pp. 189–219; and Anthony Wilden, *The Language of the Self* (Baltimore, 1968), which includes a translation of Lacan's "The Function of Language in Psychoanalysis," along with a detailed commentary by Wilden.
30. See Habermas, "Toward a Theory of Communicative Competence," in H. P. Dreitzel, ed., *Recent Sociology No. 2: Patterns of Communicative Behavior* (New York, 1970), esp. pp. 117–29.
31. Claus Mueller, "Notes on the Repression of Communicative Behavior," in ibid., p. 105.

32. Habermas, "Psychoanalysis and Social Theory," p. 276.

33. Ibid.

34. Philip Slater, *The Pursuit of Loneliness* (Boston, 1970), p. 125.

35. Habermas, "Psychoanalysis and Social Theory," p. 279. More generally, throughout this chapter my representation of Habermas' reconceptualization of critical theory is heavily indebted to Trent Schroyer's forthcoming study, *The Critique of Domination*.

36. In this respect the "Habermasian" interpretation of the dynamics of institutionalization seems to converge with that of Paul Cardan, who (in his article, "Marxisme et theorie revolutionnaire," *Socialisme ou Barbarie*, no. 39, pp. 60–61), building on the theories of Jacques Lacan, defines the institution as "a symbolic, socially sanctioned network in which a functional and an imaginary component combine in varying proportions and relationships." See also René Lourau, "Marxisme et institutions," *l'Homme et la Société*, no. 14 (October–November–December 1969).

37. Habermas, "Psychoanalysis and Social Theory," p. 276.

38. Ibid., p. 279.

39. Pierre Fougeyrollas, *La révolution freudienne* (Paris, 1970), p. 87.

40. Erich Fromm, "The Dogma of Christ," in *The Dogma of Christ and Other Essays* (New York, 1963), p. 20.

41. Ibid.

42. Henri Lefebvre, *Everyday Life in the Modern World* (London, 1971), p. 146.

43. Ibid.

44. See Herbert Marcuse, "The Affirmative Character of Culture," in *Negations: Essays in Critical Theory* (Boston, 1968), p. 95.

45. Fromm, "Psychoanalytic Characterology and Its Relevance for Social Psychology," in *The Crisis of Psychoanalysis*, p. 153.

46. Mueller, "Notes on the Repression of Communicative Behavior," p. 104.

47. Lefebvre, *Everyday Life in the Modern World*, p. 146.

48. Habermas, "Psychoanalysis and Social Theory," p. 280.

49. Paul Baran and Paul Sweezy, *Monopoly Capital* (New York, 1966), p. 352.
50. Habermas, "Psychoanalysis and Social Theory," p. 280.
51. Ibid.
52. Ibid.

4

Revolution and Counter-Revolution in Late Capitalist Society

Inasmuch as the new critical theory succeeded in placing the sociocultural tendencies of modern capitalism within the context of a new totalization uniting the dialectics of psychic life and their reciprocal relations with the dialectics of historical life, it provided a unique basis for renovation of the Marxist theory of class struggle and revolution in the light of the problematic posed by the post-World War II evolution of civilization. The nature of this problematic has already been discussed in our introductory chapter. It may briefly be restated here in terms of the two basic hypotheses of historical materialism: that no society sets itself tasks until it has produced the means for their solution, and that no society disappears before it has exhausted all of its potentialities. As Antonio Gramsci so lucidly noted in the 1920s, while "vulgar Marxism" has customarily *identified* these two propositions *with one another,* in fact there is a profound *disjunction* between the two which expresses itself as a sort of polar oscillation within the historical process. The key to the understanding of the process of historical change and social transformation is to be found in the analysis of this disjunction within the framework of historical materialism. Far from allowing us simply to formulate some conception of the "general laws of history" and thereby to dispense with

101

the concrete analysis of particular historical conjunctures within the development of the class struggle, the perspective of the new critical theory forces us continually to update our analysis in the light of every new development.[1] Indeed, it is only on the basis of such an analysis that it becomes possible even to identify the alignment of social forces—of antagonistic classes—at any particular moment. For once the essential complexity of the processes of historical change is grasped, it becomes clear that the class struggle never presents itself in the form of a simple polar opposition between bourgeoisie and proletariat, rulers and masses, as defined by the fundamental societal contradiction between capital and labor. The "people" or "masses" never constitute a stable, objective category, but rather correspond to an identity that is mutable and conjunctural, continually being redefined through the actual historical course of social practice.

Lenin and Trotsky provided a tentative approach to this problem through their law of combined and uneven development as it applied to social structure and economic development (i.e., as regards the unevenness of quantitative economic growth, the uneven rationality of this growth, the lags and distortions between sectors of economic life, and between economic development as a whole and social institutions).[2] Through this analysis of the combined and uneven development of contradictions and their "overdetermination" on a global scale, Leninism attempted to locate the "weakest links" of the whole imperialist system at any given moment. In contrast, the new critical theory suggested the need to extend the principle of combined and uneven development beyond the socioeconomic terrain, to encompass the spheres of the "superstructures," of culture, everyday life, etc., and the different levels of consciousness.

Given the broader formulation of the law of uneven development implicit in the Freudo-Marxist synthesis, it becomes apparent that not only do the development of particular institutional or cultural spheres, the psychic make-up of specific groups, or the modes of everyday life and interaction not necessarily progress in a direction and at a tempo identical to that of material production, but also these "superstructural" elements need not *absolutely* reflect material constraints but may to some degree contain a spiritual denial of these constraints and may therefore anticipate their eventual disappearance.[3] Within this analysis it becomes clear that it is necessary to extend the notion of contradiction to account for the possibility of specific contradictions over and beyond the system's fundamental contradiction between productive forces and social relations —contradictions which manifest themselves *within* and *between* each of these sectors and which may in turn give rise to new sources of social conflict and historical transformation. It is also true that the analysis of this unevenness between the temporality of different subsystems within the overall historical movement of social and cultural systems also requires the employment of a conception of the ambivalence of these disjunctions—that is, of the extent to which such lags and disjunctions between subsystems may interact to cancel out such secondary contradictions rather than to reinforce them and strengthen the system's coherence or facilitate the reproduction of structures which might otherwise be threatened with disintegration. As regards the latter instance, it could be argued, for example, that just as we are familiar with the extent to which, on the level of the world economy, colonization and underdevelopment represent two sides of the same process—a process through which imperialistic capitalism attempts to utilize regional dispro-portionalities in development to rationalize itself and to attenuate its economic contradictions by creating satellitic economies and administered markets—so also does this process operate on the level of everyday life within the metropolitan countries in the artificial preservation of retrograde areas and archaic forms in the interests of power. Despite the rise of classical capitalism in the nineteenth century, according to Horkheimer:

> The family remained essentially a feudal institution based on the principle of "blood" and thus was thoroughly irrational, whereas an industrialist society (though itself including irrational elements in its very essence) proclaims rationality, the exclusive rule of the principle of calculability and of free exchange following nothing but [the law of] supply and demand. The modern family owes its social significance as well as its inner difficulties to this inconsistency. . . . There is no bourgeois family in the strictest sense of the word; in itself it is a contradiction of the principle of individualism—and yet a necessary one. Since the period of its emancipation, it has assumed a pseudo-feudal, hierarchical structure. Man liberated from serfdom in alien households became the master in his own. Children, for whom the world had been a penitentiary throughout the Middle Ages, continued to be slaves well into the nineteenth century.[4]

Far from being a mere accidental anachronism, this tenacious survival of a family "whose binary structure escapes regulation by the equivalency of exchange"[5] and which preserves direct personal dependence in the home long after the bourgeois separation of state and society, of political and private life, is completed, is in fact a vital necessity for the reproduction of capitalist social relations. Along with countless other pre-capitalist remnants or enclaves which have survived within developed bourgeois society, it constitutes an irrationality necessary for the preservation of a society which is rational in its means but not in its ends. As hierarchical power and commodity relations colonize the everyday life of a society, the most ancient of institutions—such as the family or institutionalized religion—while on a certain level remaining philosophically opposed to the more modern institutions of political and economic life, nevertheless are artificially forced into complementary and symbiotic relationships with the latter. As Henri Lefebvre has put it:

> The first repress desire, the second take care of needs; the first establish order in the unconscious, the others in consciousness; [thus] the more ancient institutions have refined their displays and practices in accordance with the "depth" they administer, while maintaining a befitting detachment from worldly matters, whereas the others aim at what is on the surface, [at] physical activities (consumption, everyday life, etc.); [finally,] the "spiritual" institutions direct the private life of each individual (their policy being to terrorize sexuality), while the rule of the modern institutions spreads terror in everyday life.[6]

It is precisely this process of intervention by hierarchical power in everyday life and the colonization of its various spheres in the interests of domination which constitutes the practice of "hegemony" through which, according to Gramsci, the ruling class succeeds in supplementing its material power with forms of cultural and institutional domination that are, in the last instance, even more crucial to the preservation of class rule than mere coercive force.[7] Inasmuch as such interventions succeed in reestablishing the coherence of culture and everyday life, which the tendency of capitalist development to universalize the commodity form would otherwise destroy, the chronic sectoral imbalances and secondary contradictions within and between the various sectors which express the objective irrationalities of capitalist development, instead of coalescing in their efforts to sharpen the antagonisms between classes within this system, will rather overdetermine each other in such a way as to obscure and diffuse those conflicts. In this way, the practice of bourgeois hegemony serves to recuperate all those tendencies within everyday life that tend toward independence, and which might otherwise have become part of the forces that would destroy the system of class power, and thus, subjectively, to cement the society together in the face of objective tendencies toward its disintegration. It follows that in opposition to the practice of hegemony, revolutionary practice must equally base itself on a comprehension of the interaction between the simultaneous and opposed regularities characterizing the various spheres of culture and everyday life so as to dissolve the pseudo-coherence imposed on these spheres by class power and hence to undermine the questionable claims of objectively anachronistic power to legitimacy within such institutions. Such a practice would reverse the hierarchy of mediations between the different levels or contexts making up social life and provide the basis for a new unification of objective and subjective processes in the form of a counter-hegemonic force.

Such a cultural revolutionary analysis and practice, based on a dialectical comprehension of the role of particular cultural and institutional spheres and their changing interrelationships in the maintenance or dissolution of a given form of society, is not equally meaningful at all periods of history; nor is the necessity for such an intervention in these processes equally apparent at every point in space and time throughout the history of the class struggle. There are some moments when a catastrophic conjuncture of circumstances creates a revolutionary situation, as in Russia in 1917, or when the abrupt collapse of a specific mode of economic organization has so undermined the existing forms of institutional authority and cultural legitimation "that the needs of the greater part of society easily turn into rebellion." [8] But, as Horkheimer noted in 1934, "such moments are rare and brief: the decaying order is quickly improved where necessary and is apparently renewed; the periods of restoration last a long time, and during them the outmoded cultural apparatus as well as the psychic make-up of men and the body of interconnected institutions acquire new power." ⁹ During such brief moments of social and political disintegration in which the simple instinct for survival is sufficient to mobilize the masses into opposition, a resolute minority, like the Bolshevik party, may succeed in exploiting the situation by overthrowing the power of an old ruling class temporarily stripped of its ideological legitimacy. But in the absence of any subsequent "deep-reaching change in the emotional and instinctual life" of the masses, the same process of restoration is inevitable despite the intentions of the revolutionary leadership; the survival of authoritarian traits in the masses' psychic make-up becomes the basis for a "return of the repressed" through the reproduction of correspondingly authoritarian institutions and thus of a new ruling class as well.

And so, despite the destruction of the Czarist regime and the seizure of power by a revolutionary minority in Russia in the name of a communist transformation of society, the psychic structure and capacity for freedom of the working masses were too inhibited for them to carry through with the revolutionary mission assigned to them by Marxist theory and reconfirmed in Lenin's *State and Revolution*—that is, for these masses themselves actively to reorganize and manage the productive forces. To do so would have required a dramatic transformation of their authoritarian psychic make-up, but the Bolshevik leaders neither understood the psychological and sexual roots of these authoritarian traits nor, consequently, what forces might have been utilized to facilitate the creation of structures capable of free self-regulation. Such a cultural revolution, as Reich recognized, requires at the very minimum a radical transformation both of the prevailing relations between men and women and, above all, of the forms of familial life, especially as regards their socializing functions. More specifically, concerning the need for a new familial structure, as Agnes Heller and Mihály

Vajda have suggested, for a revolutionary solution to this problem to be meaningful it must incorporate at least the following features:

> (1) It must be a democratically structured community which allows the early learning of democratic propensities. (2) It must guarantee many-sided human relations, including those between children and adults. (3) It must guarantee the development and realization of individuality—the basic pre-condition of this [being] the free choosing and re-choosing of human ties even in childhood. (4) It must eliminate both the conflicts originating in monogamy and those originating in its dissolution.[10]

It is true that the Bolsheviks, following Engels in his identification of the patriarchal family and monogamous marriage with private property and class domination, abolished all the old family laws of the Czarist regime and decreed both the equality of women and a program for their immediate full entrance into economic life.* At the same time, however, lacking any real comprehension of the profound psychosexual functions of the family and its role in the formation of the individual's psychic make-up, they were unable to put forth a coherent program for the creation of forms of non-compulsive self-regulation to replace the old

---

* In Alexandra Kollontai's *Communism and the Family* it is recognized that the construction of a socialist society necessarily involves not simply the creation of formal equality between women and men but also women's economic independence from men and from the compulsions that economic dependence on men made inevitable. It followed from this argument (which, along with Riazanov's essay on *Communisme et mariage*, marks the high point of Bolshevik reflection on these problems) that housekeeping and other domestic duties must be socialized and mechanized so as to no longer monopolize the time of women or stifle their creative self-expression. Similarly, the upbringing of children was to be increasingly entrusted to nurseries, kindergartens, and other communal institutions.[11]

family and the old morality. Nor did they understand the emotionally explosive and socially dangerous potential contained in the profound contradiction between the disintegration of old forms of family life and sexual morality, and the fact that the new revolutionary society was composed mainly of former family members whose psychic structures were thus formed almost exclusively within the rigidly patriarchal environment of the Czarist era.*

Thus, while in September 1919 Lenin could truthfully state that "in the Soviet Republic not a stone remains of the laws which [once] confined women to an inferior status," [13] and while it was also true that the patriarchal family had been legally abolished, the attitudes and motivational structures on which the oppression of women and patriarchal authority were based persisted. As a consequence, the new ways of living—the new relationships between men and women and between parents and children—instead of anchoring themselves in the psychic structures of the masses, came into increasingly intense conflict with the old, compulsive, patricentric values of these masses, rooted as they were in the old ways of living.[14] Lacking a theoretical perspective or analysis capable of comprehending these constraints on the development of "the revolution in the cultural superstructure," and further constrained by the scars of their own

---

* It was, for instance, not recognized to what extent the success of Makarenko's experiments in communally socializing children was largely dependent on the fact that these children (who were, for the most part, orphans of the civil war who had banded together in semi-wild gangs in order to survive during the period of disorder) had uniquely escaped the formative influences of the pre-revolutionary family. As a consequence, the initial optimism which the Bolsheviks derived from this experiment with regard to the prospects for "forging a new man," as Makarenko put it, was shortly to prove to be misplaced when put to the test of the much more deeply rooted patriarchal values and authoritarian traits characterizing the vast majority of the Russian population.[12]

repressive socialization, the Bolsheviks tended to follow the course of least resistance. They talked about revolutionizing everyday life without actually examining the reality of this life. They inevitably came to misinterpret the existing chaos of everyday life as a "moral crisis" (using the term in exactly the same sense as the representatives of political reaction), instead of comprehending it as the necessarily chaotic accompaniment to a profound transformation of a whole way of living. As a result—albeit in the face of economic difficulties and a virtual state of siege imposed by the imperialist powers—they became ever more conservative. Conscious steps were taken to restore or strengthen the compulsive family structure and ultimately to reinstitute the most repressive aspects of bourgeois sexual morality as well. Lenin, for instance, denounced the youth movement as being "exaggeratedly concerned with sex"; the younger generation, he argued, had been infected "by the disease of modernity in its attitude towards sexual questions." [15] By 1934, the legal prohibition on homosexuality was reintroduced in the USSR, and two years later abortions were similarly prohibited.

The consequences of these constraints on the revolution in the cultural superstructure and of this restoration of the family and the patriarchal ideology were, of course, not confined to the immediate sphere of domestic life. In the absence of a deep-reaching effect on the masses' emotional and instinctual life, such as could only have been provided by a new way of socializing children and a new type of sexual morality, the Bolshevik seizure of power and the subsequent replacement of the control of individual capitalists over production with a system of rational state planning, "has not in the least altered the typical, helpless and authoritarian character structure of the [Russian] masses." [16] In this sense, the inhibition of the sexual and cultural revolution, in addition to perpetuating the subordination of women and children, also served profoundly to reinforce the tendencies toward authoritarianism throughout Soviet society. As Trotsky pointed out in 1936, the most compelling motive for the revival of the cult of the family and of patriarchal authority was "undoubtedly the need of the bureaucracy for a stable hierarchy of relations and for the disciplining of youth by means of 40 million points of support for authority and power." [17] Regardless of the nature of the revolutionary program and ideology, the persistence of authoritarian structures in the masses nullified all attempts at establishing or maintaining organizations run along truly democratic principles. As a consequence, it necessarily fell to the state and party bureaucracies to carry out the tasks that Marx's revolutionary project had reserved for the proletarian masses —whose mental structures and capacity for self-regulation were too inhibited to respond to the rapid development of social and economic organization.

Subsequent attempts to create socialist regimes on the Soviet model, most notably in Eastern Europe, have exhibited the same regressive tendencies. Despite the seizure of state power, the revolution in the cultural superstructure has nowhere taken place, "because the bearer and guardian of this revolution, the psychic structure of human beings, was not changed." [18] In every case, the compulsive family structure and patriarchal ideology have only been modified in regard to those aspects which are directly connected to a specifically bourgeois mode of domination, while the general mechanisms through which these institutions reproduce domination have been left substantially untouched. Similarly, in every instance the shaping of the new man necessary for the formation of a new society has been dealt with entirely in terms of authoritarian models of socialization,[19] which seek to change the *content* of education by teaching certain socialist principles but in no way modify the "top-down" *forms* of education in the direction of greater autonomy at the base. However notably such revolutions may succeed on the higher level by eliminating the bourgeois system of property relations, inasmuch as they all continue to put off the "human dimension" by leaving intact the repressive morality of everyday life they can easily accommodate themselves to almost every form of psychological and cultural degeneration—to the revival of the patriarchal family, to sexual repression, to the repressive organization of the school, etc.—and, along with the preservation of these mechanisms for internalizing reactionary ideologies in the character structure of the masses, there come the inevitable processes of political and social degeneration—for instance, the depoliticization and atomization of the masses, leading, as in Russia, to the replacement of proletarian democracy by bureaucratic efficiency, of Lenin by Stalin.*

The failure of the Bolshevik revolution to develop the Soviet masses' capacity for freedom—for the conscious self-management of production and self-regulation of everyday life—was in part due to the objective immaturity of the productive forces in Russia, which condemned the revolutionary regime to undertake under state auspices the process

---

* Although this tendency toward a return of the repressed is manifested in its most extreme form in the Stalinist period in the USSR, it follows that the Russian experience is not the exception but the rule in the state socialist countries. Even in Cuba it is possible to discern a distressing tendency toward the bureaucratic degeneration of the regime as the original revolutionary *élan* of the early years wanes and, with this regression, a parallel tendency toward the reinstitution of a repressive morality in the sphere of everyday life—a morality which serves to sanctify sexual repression, to preserve monogamy, to perpetuate the enslavement of women, and to encourage the suppression of homosexuals. Similarly, in China we find sexual repression taken to an extreme which, in its almost total obliteration of any living sexuality, suggests the reincarnation of the puritanism of the seventeenth-century bourgeoisie in a new collective form.[20]

of industrial accumulation already carried out in the West by the bourgeoisie. In fact, Lenin had looked to the triumph of the revolutionary struggle in the more advanced capitalist West as the indispensable means of overcoming the inevitable constraints placed on the development of communism by Russia's backwardness. Yet the later 1920s and the 1930s saw not only the degeneration of Soviet democracy into Stalinism but the simultaneous failure of the revolutionary movement in the West to culminate in the development of the *subjective* preconditions among the masses for the transition to a socialist organization of society, despite the presence throughout these countries of the *objective* basis—indeed, the objective necessity—for this transition. Rather than responding to events such as the two world wars and the Great Depression, which so clearly demonstrated the obsolescence and moral bankruptcy of bourgeois social relations, with a rational assertion of their own self-interest, the masses surrendered instead to a politics of unreason and disaster which was the very antithesis of their interest. Clearly, such a phenomenon required—even more urgently than did the catastrophe of Stalinism—an analysis which did not rest content with merely establishing the objective basis of social movements but which comprehended all the cultural and characterological processes which mediated between these objective tendencies and contradictions and their actual coming-to-consciousness.

The analysis of fascism and other modes of late-capitalist domination within this perspective in no way rejects the more orthodox Marxist interpretation of these phenomena as political responses to a new stage in the development of the capitalist system in which monopoly has replaced competition and in which, in order to attenuate the increasingly intense contradictions of economic overproduction and instability which accompany this transformation, the preservation of class power becomes ever more dependent on aggressive economic expansion and militarism abroad and the increasing replacement of liberal parliamentarianism by more direct forms of class dictatorship at home. As Horkheimer put it, "He who will not speak of capitalism, should also be silent about fascism." [21] Although in certain respects this development necessitated a rupture with the rational legitimations of the liberal market system and laissez-faire state, and its replacement by a system of *"Gangsterherrschaft"*—that is, by an openly terroristic dictatorship of the most reactionary elements, which lacks any rational justification—at the same time it also represented on another level a logical extension of tendencies already present in the liberal system. As Marcuse argued in "The Struggle Against Liberalism in the Totalitarian View of the State," [22] the transition "from the liberalist to the total-authoritarian state occurs within the framework of a single social order." In particular, fascism has its most fundamental source in "the naturalistic interpretation of society and the liberalist rationalism that ends in irrationalism." [23] The liberal rationalization of the capitalist economic and social order was essentially restricted to the private sphere (to the practice of the individual in the market system); to extend this criterion of rationality to the public sphere (to the determination of social goals) would directly call into question the privileges of a ruling class dependent upon the private appropriation of production. Accordingly, when the obsolescence of the competitive mechanisms of the free market, as a consequence of the growing predominance of monopolistic organization, demands the systematic intervention of public power in order to offset the tendency of late capitalism to chronic economic depression, the liberal mythology of the harmony of interests collapses as a means of legitimating privilege and power and it becomes necessary to seek irrational justifications for capitalist rule. Thus, with regard to the question of the continuity of the socioeconomic base, we can say that "liberalism" produces the total-authoritarian state out of itself, as its own consummation at a more advanced stage of development. Despite all changes, the certainty of profit, for instance, remains the underlying motive of the system as much in its fascist as in its liberal phase. Where, for example, fascist ideology seems to be attacking the idea of private appropriation, it is in fact only directing this attack against the practice of the bourgeoisie of the competitive era.

This analysis of the objective tendencies within capitalism that underlay the transformation of the liberal order into the fascist system, while necessary to any valid understanding of these phenomena, was not, from the standpoint of the new critical theory, sufficient to such an understanding. While it could account for the willingness of the bourgeoisie to abandon liberalism and embrace authoritarian forms of class dictatorship, it failed to comprehend the subjective tendencies in culture and in the psychic make-up of various groups which made it possible for this bourgeoisie to find a mass base for its coup d'état. It was all well and good for orthodox Marxists to talk of fascism as a conspiracy of the great monopoly capitalists who exploited the prejudices, values, and ideological convictions of the masses for its own ends, but monopoly capitalism cannot create the beliefs and emotions it exploits out of nothing; nor does it necessarily control all the future actions of the movement it has brought to power. In contrast to such conspiratorial or economistic interpretations, which served only to obscure the actual situation and alignment of forces confronting the left at the time and hence to disarm its attempts to rally the proletariat against the fascist menace, the Frankfurt Marxists in particular insisted on the need to comprehend the cultural sources of fascism and the precedents for fascist moralism contained within the affirmative culture of the preceding era with its characteristic bourgeois hostility to happiness.[24]

In the pre-fascist period, this culture was characterized by the "internalization" by each individual, in the form of an ascetic ideal of duty and service, of the desire for sensuous gratification and happiness. Under fascism, this ideal of duty and service to the totality at the sacrifice of individual happiness is not abandoned but only finds expression in a new form. The abstract "internal" community (abstract because it left all the real, crucial antagonisms through which capitalist domination was expressed—such as the oppositions between individual and society, private and public life, law and morality, economics and politics—unresolved except on a purely spiritual level) is transformed into an equally abstract "external community." In this way, the spiritual and moral vacuum created by the development of bourgeois society and by the progress of rationalization and secularization inherent in the liberal program leads the individual to seek recompense from all the still unresolved oppositions of the liberalistic era by inserting her/himself into false collectivities based on a regressive identification with the group in terms of a symbolic community of race, folk, blood, soil, etc.[25] In this respect, for Horkheimer and Theodor Adorno, fascist anti-semitism is simply an index of the more general tendency toward stereotypical thought in late capitalism which arises as the intensified contradictions of this system expose the liberal principle of the potential unity of mankind as a fraud under the prevailing socioeconomic conditions. No longer able to tolerate the dichotomies between inner and outer, appearance and essence, individual fate and social reality, the mass individual thus seeks harmony through the sacrifice of his or her autonomy, with individual projections being replaced by collective ones, such as anti-semitism, racism, xenophobia, etc.[26]

In all these ways, then, despite the collapse of the liberal market as a self-regulating system of economic exchanges and a fundamental integrative mechanism of the classical system, the potentialities latent in this disintegrative process for the development of revolutionary consciousness among the masses were subject to inhibitions in the cultural sphere. This cultural sphere maintained its unity as an integrative system of substitute gratifications and hence was able to function as an instrument of adaptation by which the decaying economic order was restored and its disrupted links with the summits of institutional power reconnected. Yet this manipulation of cultural legitimations, by which political reaction sought to insulate itself against the tendencies toward the dissolution of institutional authority generated by the economic crisis, would still have been meaningless had it not struck a responsive chord in the psychic make-up of the masses, who felt the burden of this decline in economic life most sharply. The problem is not that "political reaction, with fascism and the church at its head, demands that the masses renounce happiness here on earth" in the name of duty, self-denial, and sacrifice for the fatherland, but rather, as Reich pointed out, "that the masses, by complying with these demands, are supporting the reactionaries and allowing them to enrich themselves and extend their power." [27] To understand how this was made possible it was necessary, according to the Freudo-Marxists, to extend the analysis yet one step further. It had to account for the effect of these economic disruptions and cultural transformations on the characterological structures of the social groups making up society and the manner in which they facilitated the surrender of these masses to a politics which, instead of constituting a rational affirmation of their human interests, based itself on appeals to their latent death wishes, their ingrained guilt feelings, their willingness to bear inordinate sacrifices silently and sometimes even happily.

Such an analysis would begin with the recognition that against every manifestation of a will to freedom, a desire for happiness, that emerges within the mass individual in such situations, must be set the inertia of deeply entrenched

characterological structures which serve to suppress these
impulses. Thus, "if one investigates ecclesiastical, fascist and
other reactionary ideologies for their unconscious content,"
noted Reich, "one finds that they are essentially defense
reactions . . . formed for fear of the unconscious inferno
which everyone carries within himself." [28] Or, as Fromm put
it in *Escape from Freedom*, "if the economic, social, and
political conditions on which the whole process of human
individuation depends, do not offer a basis for the realization
of individuality . . . , while at the same time, people have
lost those ties which gave them security, this lag makes
freedom an unbearable burden." [29] In the years following
World War I, this feeling, which is at the root of the masses'
"fear of freedom," was being intensified by the further
development of monopoly capitalism, and with it the growth
of new forms of social integration characteristic of the
so-called mass society. The spread of bureaucratic rationality
and individuation, along with the breakdown of the primary
links in the traditional patterns of life and community, gave
rise to all the mass-psychological strains familiar in such a
society: feelings of alienation, isolation, insecurity, and fear.
As a result of the emergence of a society dominated by giant
corporations and the decreasing importance or disappear-
ance of intermediate structures, "the individual's feeling of
powerlessness and aloneness has increased, his 'freedom'
from all traditional bonds has become more pronounced, his
possibilities for individual economic achievement have nar-
rowed down, [and] he feels threatened by gigantic forces." [30]
The more the contradictions in society grow, the blinder and
more uncontrollable the social forces become, the more
catastrophes such as war and unemployment overshadow the
life of the individual, and the stronger and more widespread
becomes the tendency for the individual to respond to
his/her isolation and insecurity through various destructive
defense mechanisms, all of which accentuate the irrational,

destructive, and authoritarian tendencies within the average character structure.

This authoritarian mass individual is still essentially the anal-obsessive personality type that is characteristic of classical capitalism. But whereas this type was originally most characteristic and most highly developed among the bourgeoisie, with the transition from classical to monopoly capitalism it becomes less and less a characteristic of the bourgeoisie (for whom it is no longer really functional) and more and more the property of the petty bourgeoisie. In terms of its socializing functions, the typical petty-bourgeois family reflects the external pressures felt in general by members of this stratum (which is almost totally bereft of the independence that had previously been the most distinctive feature of the bourgeoisie) in the tendency for the old anal-obsessive type increasingly to regress toward what Fromm has called the "authoritarian-masochistic character." Anxious about status, rigidly adhering to values it no longer feels spontaneously, this sort of family typically overcompensates by almost frantically reinforcing an authoritarian structure which increasingly appears irrational. The more the economic and social functions of the family are liquidated, the more desperately it stresses its outmoded, conventional forms, and with this regression in its structure, the more it tends to reproduce unstable, yet increasingly authoritarian, personality types.[31]

Politically, this authoritarian-masochistic type, under the pressures of economic insecurity, increasing monopolization, and the status-anxiety brought on by the threat of proletarianization, may increasingly tend to abandon the individualistic conservatism of the older bourgeoisie in search of more extreme panaceas. "A serf who rebels and yet remains a serf," he or she is in part searching for a new authority to replace the weakened father image which increasingly lacks any true inner authority. Fascist politics and propaganda, as Reich showed, served in turn to channel the anxiety generated by the crises of private and familial life so as to effectively mobilize large sections of the masses toward counter-revolutionary ends. Familial fixations—rooted, in the case of women, in fear of sexual freedom and of the dissolution of monogamous security; in the case of the young, in Oedipal guilt; and in the case of adult males, in the threatening specter represented by the disintegration of patriarchal authority with all its implications in terms of unconscious fears of castration, etc.—are all reinforced in such a way as to strengthen the emotional basis of the prevailing authoritarian system. The tendency toward infantile regression and toward anal-obsessive patterns that typically accompanies this process of reaction formation renders the masses especially susceptible to propaganda appealing to unconscious orgiastic yearnings and to identification with a "Führer-figure" whose "love for the people" serves them as a substitute for any real satisfaction of their needs:

> I have tried to show in Hitler's writings the two trends that we have already described as fundamental for the authoritarian character: the craving for power over men and the longing for submission to an overwhelmingly strong outside power. Hitler's ideas are more or less identical with the ideology of the Nazi party. . . . This ideology results from his personality which, with its inferiority feeling, hatred against life, asceticism, and envy of those who enjoy life, is the soil of sado-masochistic strivings; it was addressed to people who, on account of their similar character structure, felt attracted and excited by these teachings and became ardent followers of the man who expressed what they felt. But it was not only the Nazi ideology that satisfied the lower middle class; the political practice realized what the ideology promised. A hierarchy was created in which everyone had somebody above him to submit to and somebody beneath him to feel power over; the man at the top, the leader, has Fate, History, Nature

above him as the power in which to submerge himself. Thus the Nazi ideology and practice satisfies the desires springing from the character structure of one part of the population and gives direction and orientation to those who, though not enjoying domination and submission, were resigned and had given up faith in life, in their own decisions, in everything.[32]

Although, to be sure, it was the petty bourgeoisie which exhibited these characteristics in their most pronounced form, and which therefore formed the mass basis for the fascist counter-revolution, it is also undeniable that many aspects of the authoritarian-masochistic syndrome also characterized the psychic structure of the working class itself. This was, in fact, shown empirically by a study of authoritarian tendencies in the German proletariat carried out in the beginning of the 1930s by Erich Fromm and E. Schachtel under the sponsorship of the Institut für Sozialforschung in Frankfurt.[33] Starting from the observation that on the surface, the working class in 1930 appeared, according to such indices as their preferences in political and shop steward elections, to be solidly opposed to fascism and on the side of democracy, this study attempted to explore the actual psychological depth of this anti-fascist commitment in order to determine the potential resistance to the ever growing threat of a fascist coup. As Fromm put it:

The question we asked at the time was: to what extent do German workers and employees have a character structure which is opposite to the authoritarian idea of Nazism? And it implied still another question: to what extent will the German workers and employees, in the critical hour, fight Nazism? . . . A study was made, and the result was that, roughly speaking, 10% of the German workers and employees had what we call an authoritarian character structure, about 15% had a democratic character structure, and the vast majority— about 75%—were people whose character structure was a mixture of both extremes. The theoretical assumption was that the authoritarians would be ardent Nazis, the "demo-cratic" ones militant anti-Nazis, and that the majority would be neither one nor the other. These theoretical assumptions turned out to be more or less accurate, as events in the years between 1933 and 1945 showed.[34]

It follows from this analysis that the failure of the left to rally the masses against fascist reaction was a direct result of its failure to comprehend the cultural factors and inner psycho-logical contradictions conditioning the response of the working class to the fascist onslaught and the socioeconomic situation in which it occurred—that is, the fact "that the revolutionary element in [the proletarian's] psychic structure was partly underdeveloped [and] partly counteracted by opposite reactionary elements in his structure." [35] Inasmuch as it was because men and women were alienated and uprooted that they so eagerly accepted the spurious ethnic community proposed by National Socialism, it also follows that these anomic phenomena might, under different circum-stances, have become sources of revolutionary struggle rather than of fascist irrationalism. That the fascists triumphed rather than the left was in the last analysis due to the fact that they understood far better than their opponents how the frustration by bourgeois social relations of all the richest emotional capabilities, the most tender impulses, and the need for community and communication, drives men and women to all the forms of religion and chauvinism, to the sentimentality of films and festivals which express in the sphere of the imagination the love they are deprived of in everyday life. Inasmuch as the same factors continue today to be responsible for the contemporary "mass" man's self-im-mersion in the trivial and meretricious culture dispensed by the mass media and by the system of mass consumption which has been created to manipulate the needs of alienated and uprooted individuals, it further follows that ignorance of the inhibitions which counteract the will to freedom as it is generated by the socioeconomic position of subordinate groups and classes in the face of the objective obsolescence of bourgeois social relations and which thus lead to irrationality instead of revolutionary praxis on the part of the masses, not only disarmed the left in the 1930s but has continued to do so up to the present day. And such cultural and psychological naivety will also bring to naught the struggles of revolutionaries in the future unless these struggles take account of what is happening "inside people's heads" and in the various spheres of culture and everyday life—that is, unless, on the basis of their understanding of the nature of "the progressive desires, ideas, and thoughts which are latent in people of different social strata, occupations, age groups, and sexes," and of the elements rooted in a thousand aspects of everyday life which "prevent the progressive desires, ideas, etc., from developing" [36] and which are incomparably stronger than mere political propaganda, they take the form of a cultural revolutionary project aimed at "the crystallizing out of the revolutionary elements in the masses." [37]

Notes

1. Antonio Gramsci, *Opere di Antonio Gramsci*, vol. 8, pp. 58–59, and vol. 4, p. 114.
2. On Lenin's use of this concept see Henri Lefebvre, *Pour connaitre la pensée de Lénine* (Paris, 1957), esp. pp. 230–48; and Louis Althusser, "Lenin and Philosophy," in *Lenin and Philosophy and Other Essays*, pp. 23–70.
3. Both Henri Lefebvre and Louis Althusser have reached (in this respect) similar conclusions: see the former's *Critique de la vie quotidienne*, 2 vols. (Paris, 1958 and 1961) and the latter's essay on "Contradiction and Overdetermination," in *For Marx* (New York, 1970).
4. Max Horkheimer, "Authority and the Family Today," in Ruth

Nanda Anshen, *The Family: Its Function and Destiny* (New York, 1949), pp. 359–60.

5. T. W. Adorno, "Society," *Salmagundi* (Winter 1969), p. 149.

6. Lefebvre, *Everyday Life in the Modern World*, pp. 160–61.

7. On Gramsci's concept of hegemony, see John Merrington, "Theory and Practice in Gramsci's Marxism," *Socialist Register 1968* (New York, 1968), pp. 145–76; Jean-Marc Piotte, *La pensée politique de Gramsci* (Paris, 1970); Carl Boggs, "Gramsci's Prison Notebooks," *Socialist Revolution*, no. 11 (September–October 1972), pp. 79–118.

8. Horkheimer, "Authority and the Family," p. 59.

9. Ibid. pp. 59–60.

10. Agnes Heller and Mihály Vajda, "Family Structure and Communism," *Telos*, no. 7 (Spring 1971), p. 106.

11. See Alexandra Kollontai, *Communism and the Family* (Bristol, England: Falling Wall Press, 1972) and D. Riazanov, *Communisme et mariage* (French translation; Paris, 1927).

12. Heller and Vajda, "Family Structure and Communism," p. 105.

13. Quoted by Maurice Brinton in *Authoritarian Conditioning, Sexual Repression and the Irrational in Politics*, p. 29.

14. See Wilhelm Reich, *The Sexual Revolution*, esp. pp. 153–211.

15. Quoted by Brinton, *Authoritarian Conditioning*, p. 33.

16. Reich, Preface to the Third Edition, *The Mass Psychology of Fascism* (New York, 1945), p. xxiii.

17. Leon Trotsky, *The Revolution Betrayed* (1936); quoted in Brinton, *Authoritarian Conditioning*, p. 37.

18. Reich, *The Sexual Revolution*, p. 159.

19. See Heller and Vajda, "Family Structure and Communism," p. 105.

20. See Kostas Axelos, "Sur la révolution sexuelle," *Praxis*, no. 3–4 (1970), pp. 457–67.

21. Max Horkheimer, "Die Juden und Europa," *Zeitschrift für Sozialforschung* (1939), p. 115.

22. Translated in *Negations*, pp. 3–42.

23. Ibid., p. 12. See also in this regard Horkheimer's "Egoismus und Freiheitsbewegung," in *Zeitschrift für Sozialforschung* (1936).

24. See Marcuse's "The Affirmative Concept of Culture," in *Negations*, pp. 88–133.

25. Ibid., p. 125.

26. See "Elements of Anti-Semitism," in Max Horkheimer and T. W. Adorno, *Dialectic of Enlightenment* (New York, 1972), pp. 168–208.

27. Wilhelm Reich, "What Is Class Consciousness?" (1934), *Liberation*, vol. 16, no. 5 (October 1971), p. 23.

28. Reich, *The Sexual Revolution*, p. 20.

29. Erich Fromm, *Escape from Freedom* (New York, 1941), p. 52.

30. Ibid., p. 144.

31. See Horkheimer, "Authority and the Family Today."

32. Fromm, *Escape from Freedom*, pp. 261–62.

33. Actually, the original study has never been published, reportedly due to the fact that much of the documentation was lost in the flight of the Frankfurt Marxists from Nazi Germany. The results, however, have been summarized in a number of articles by Fromm and in Martin Jay's dissertation, chapters IV and V.

34. Fromm, "The Revolutionary Character," in *The Dogma of Christ and Other Essays*, pp. 152–53.

35. Wilhelm Reich, *The Mass Psychology of Fascism* (New York, 1945), p. 57.

36. Reich, "What Is Class Consciousness?", p. 22.

37. Reich, *The Mass Psychology of Fascism*, p. 57.

5

Politics
Redefined

The traditional Marxist left, as we have seen, was unable to develop a critical theory of late capitalist society and an analysis capable of accounting for the relative ease with which the rulers of Western societies had repeatedly been able to enroll the masses in causes fundamentally opposed to their own basic, human interests. As a consequence of these failures, it was equally incapable of articulating a new revolutionary politics based on a recognition of the forces existing within these societies that might be utilized to combat these tendencies toward irrationalism and to give an impetus to a transformation of the masses' character structure that would render them capable of performing the social act of revolution. This is scarcely surprising, given the conditions which had determined this left's formation and development. To be sure, there was in Marx's work a general theory of the practice through which people create the conditions for a liberated existence, and a conception of the proletariat not merely as a revolutionary class but as one which by abolishing classes per se had as its mission the establishment of these conditions for a liberated individual existence. Nevertheless, as we have already suggested, at least in regard to the main corpus of Marx's writings the theory of individual emancipation remains in fact a class theory,

126

grasping only those aspects of the individual's existence which pertain to his/her economic position. It therefore puts the emphasis almost exclusively on those aspects of alienation to which the individual is subject as a direct result of the economic practice of the dominant class:

> The Marxist theory of society presupposes an immediate connection between the structure of personality and the totality of social relations. It assumes as natural that the transformation of the production and property relations, political structures, etc., of a given society will produce the type of man adequate to the new society, [but it] does not [attempt to] examine the concrete mechanisms which shape character types corresponding to social conditions.*

In short, only "those ties of character to social structure which had to be understood if the proletarians were to combine to form a class-for-itself were stressed, while the role of the individualizing and potentially liberating aspect of social relations was left to one side." [2] While this emphasis, if reductive, was nonetheless reasonable in Marx's time, "what Marx could leave aside under conditions of early capitalism was later to be actively suppressed" [3] by subsequent generations of Marxists.

For the Social Democratic parties of the Second International during the years from Marx's death to 1914, Marxism came to be identified almost exclusively with political

---

* More specifically, as Gramsci put it, "Reality is rich in bizarre combinations and it is the theoretician who must out of this confusion find the proof of his theory: e.g. translate into theoretical language the elements of historical life; not, on the contrary, the reality which must present itself in accordance with abstract schemas." This is because the conjuncture of factors determining the conditions under which the class struggle is waged is "the product of an original and unique combination which must in turn be understood and comprehended in the context of this originality if one is to dominate and overcome it." [1]

economy and with a deterministic interpretation of history of an essentially positivistic sort. Since revolution, according to this view, is essentially the outcome of an objective mechanism by which the development of the productive forces will sooner or later necessitate the transition to a new system of social relations, it requires little in the way of subjective preparation. In other words, it was assumed that such changes in the consciousness and character of the masses which might be necessary to the creation of this new system of socioeconomic organization would automatically take place as a reflection of the transformation of material processes. The mass socialist party mainly had the function of anticipating this development by constituting itself as a state-within-a-state which, when the inevitable economic crisis resulted in the disintegration of the bourgeois regime, would step into the breach and become the proletarian state. There was no recognition of the need for socialism to represent a qualitative change in human relations or for the abolition of economic alienation through societal reorganiza-tion to be accompanied by the abolition of political aliena-tion through the destruction of the state as an entity separate from and above civil society and the reappropriation of its functions by society itself. Needless to say, such a conception could only lead to an organizational life which, since it based itself on the same principles of authority, efficiency, etc., as bourgeois society, would inevitably serve to reproduce within these parties the same forms of hierarchical organization that characterized the society in general. Similarly, in the cultural sphere, while the Social Democratic organizations encour-aged separate cultural activities and talked incessantly of "proletarian culture," most of these activities were not essentially different from those of the affirmative bourgeois culture in general. The history of German Social Democracy, as Horkheimer has observed, is a perfect illustration of the dangers of such an attitude toward culture: "Instead of a critical attitude toward the dominant culture, which would have provided the only chance for the future preservation of its elements, this endeavor often only served to clothe it in the finery of the bourgeois wisdom of bygone days—much as peasants are wont to put on the outmoded fashions of their overlords." [4] As a consequence of the Social Democratic organizations' inability to transcend the dominant culture, their evolution not only tended to reproduce an imitation of the dominant culture, but ironically tended also to stabilize the culture it was supposed to supersede by diverting those energies and activities which the proletarians would otherwise have been more likely to expend in revolutionary action into forms of substitute gratification in the cultural sphere, since the dominant culture offered them no corresponding outlet for such energies.

Although, in contrast, the Bolsheviks attempted to avoid such forms of recuperation or co-optation by emphasizing not the mass base of the proletarian party but its vanguard nature, at the same time, given the beleaguered and backward state of the new revolutionary regime in Russia, it was the imperatives of toil, of sacrifice, of deferred gratification— that is, all the qualities of the anal personality and the affirmative culture, rather than those of a liberated individual and a true transcendence of repressive civilization—that prevailed. The Marxism of the vanguard, which had served to unite the revolutionary workers and peasants, was thus pressed into service as a rhetoric of duty, of the compulsive subordination of the individual to the collectivity and, ultimately, to the state. At the time of their founding, the Communist parties in the West took a more independent position, articulating, in one form or another, all the authentically revolutionary tendencies which had formerly been suppressed within Social Democracy and which only came to the fore in the great wave of spontaneous mass strikes which shook Europe following World War I. With the "Stalinization" of the Western Communist parties in the late 1920s, these tendencies once again found themselves suppressed and the Marxism of the Third International became indistinguishable from the ideology of the Soviet state. What was to some extent an unavoidable failing for the original Bolsheviks became a universal proletarian virtue for later Communists, inasmuch as they tended to base the organizational life of their respective parties, as well as their day-to-day political practice, almost exclusively on a notion of "revolutionary discipline" which was taken from the Russian model and which, under the circumstances, could only serve to reinforce all the anal-compulsive and authoritarian traits which party members had already derived from their earlier socialization. This "repressive resocialization" within the Communist left, along with all its subjective symptoms—repressed elitism, masochistic submission to authority figures, the cult of the proletariat, the growth of dogmatism—all found their objective expression in the doctrinaire forms of Marxism-Leninism which became the basic currency of international communism (and to a considerable extent, of Trotskyism as well) in these years. Michael Schneider, for one, has described the pathological syndrome by which the organizational life typical of the Leninist party serves to reinforce masochistic and authoritarian traits already present in its membership:

> The psychological symptoms of "left-wing" dogmatism and its political expressions—or rather its political symptoms—are mutually conditioning: the greater the comrades' psychological self-censorship and subjective inhibition, the more joyless their personal style of living and working, the greater will be their inclination to accept a dogmatic conception of organization and education.[5]

Such organizations, within which the members' own petty-bourgeois arrogance and elitism coexit with their equally petty-bourgeois and masochistic self-hatred as manifested in the inverted form of a "cult of the proletariat," were of course constitutionally incapable of representing the interests of the real proletariat. Furthermore, inasmuch as the authority of the elites who in the name of the revolutionary cause formed the leadership of the organization of the proletariat was dependent on their success in crippling the initiative and autonomy of the rank and file, a politics aimed at developing the spontaneous expression and self-organizational capacities of the masses would actually threaten their interests.

It is to the credit of critical Marxists like Reich or Horkheimer that they were at this time increasingly coming to recognize that as a result of these tendencies the parties of the Third International, whether in Germany or elsewhere, were no more capable than the Social Democratic parties of the Second International of serving even as instruments for the defense of the masses' existing rights—much less as agencies of revolutionary struggle. In either type of party, the community of membership, leaders, and masses as a single fighting unit was on the wane as both Communist and Social Democratic organizations were perpetuating themselves in the form of ever more authoritarian machines. Even were such machines really to attempt to represent the interests of the masses instead of the interests of their own institutional self-maintenance and organizational aggrandizement, they could not have done so, for they were no longer capable of even understanding the nature of the interests and needs of the great mass of proletarians. In short, both types of party—the mass Social Democratic party and the Bolshevik vanguard—represented equally inadequate instruments for revolutionary struggle: the mass party was not the negation of the bourgeois state but its competitor, and the vanguard party tended toward an elitism which duplicated the authoritarianism of bourgeois society. In either case, the effect of such types of politics and organization was not only to inhibit the mobilization of the masses in the face of reaction, but actually to demobilize these masses by stifling their spontaneity and virtually paving the way for the triumph of reaction. To quote Horkheimer again: "That the workers maintain an attitude of neutrality toward the totalitarian order after the betrayal of their own bureaucracy since 1914, after the development of the [proletarian] parties into world-spanning apparatuses for the destruction of spontaneity, after the murder of revolutionaries, is no sign of stupidity." [6]

It followed from this analysis that neither the means of struggle represented by the traditional forms of proletarian organization nor the ends of struggle represented by the Soviet model or by the economistic Social Democratic ideal were adequate to the tasks confronting revolutionaries. Thus, having originally built up his Sex-Pol movement as a group within the German Communist Workers' Movement (it had grown from 20,000 members to over 40,000 in the single year following its establishment in 1932), Wilhelm Reich discovered (even before his abrupt expulsion from the party in 1933) that its liberatory aims were not compatible with the forms of party politics and agitation common to the KPD and the SPD. Like other cultural revolutionaries of his time, Reich was increasingly forced to conclude that working within the existing forms of the proletarian movement and merely fighting "for improvements of propaganda in the service of old leadership" was no longer in any way desirable or useful. It had become essential to seek a constitution of the revolutionary movement on a totally new basis and, in doing so, "to find and prepare *in advance* the means which would prevent [any later] bureaucratization of a living revolutionary organization." [7] Such a new type of revolutionary movement—which would, from the start, constitute a cultural and psychological milieu favorable to the crystallization of healthy, non-authoritarian personalities and the development of a capacity for autonomous self-regulation at the base—implied a conception of the revolution as a process through which, as Horkheimer put it, "the modalities of the new society are first to be found in the course of its transformation." [8] Organization thus arises out of emancipatory praxis, as the masses reappropriate what has previously been appropriated from them—that is, as they seize control over the means of production which represents their alienated social labor, as they abolish the separation between state and society by democratically reappropriating society's alienated decision-making processes from the ruling minorities, while at the same time transforming their own inner natures so as to overcome the internalized forms of domination which block the gratification of the individual's impulses and preclude his or her self-regulation.

Implicit in this perspective was the recognition of the two-sided nature of the revolutionary process; which involves the transformation of the "inner structure" of the consciousness of the masses and requires the simultaneous revolutionization of the external world if this initial mental emancipation is to come to fruition. It implied that the struggle to overcome repressive political and economic structures must also be of such a character as to create the type of person necessary for the establishment of non-repressive forms of organization and that this necessary transformation of man and society can only be accomplished if the *conscious revolutionary intentions* of the masses are also directed toward transforming everyday life.

It was on the basis of these insights that Reich, in particular, attempted to reformulate the inherited principles of radical politics within the framework of a new, broadened conception of the revolutionary project. Although Reich accepted the macro-sociological argument of Marxism regarding the absolute necessity of overthrowing the capitalist state and the system of bourgeois property relations, he also believed it was possible to wage a struggle to subvert the reactionary influence of institutions like the family, school, and church without waiting for the great social and political revolution that would destroy the very foundations of exploitation and the need for these institutions, which manufacture ideology in the broad sense. Indeed, not only was such a struggle possible, Reich argued, but, as the fascist experience showed, it was also absolutely necessary if the struggles carried on by the left were not to provoke disastrous "defensive reactions," even fascist counter-revolution, on the part of those very masses whom the revolutionary movement claims to represent. For Reich, therefore, the principal problem faced by a cultural revolutionary politics is that of activating this passive majority of the population, which otherwise will always carry reaction to victory, through the politicization of everyday life and a struggle on this terrain to undermine those inhibitions which counteract the will to freedom that is generated in the masses by their socioeconomic subordination.

Toward this end of catalyzing a revolutionary coming-to-consciousness on the part of hitherto "non-political" masses, Reich argued in his seminal essay, "What Is Class Consciousness?" that in contrast to the abstract concern of doctrinaire Marxism with world-historical processes of socioeconomic development, for the masses the realities of capitalist social relations are immediately encountered on the more mundane levels of everyday life—that is, in the concrete problems of work, leisure, housing, family relations, neighborhood life and, of course, sexuality. Whereas for Marxism the contradiction between labor and capital exists as an objective datum, in actuality this contradiction only becomes an impetus to historical change insofar as it finds subjective expression in class consciousness and struggles—struggles which exist only insofar as there are places where there actually is a fight. Thus, although class struggle under capitalism is possible virtually everywhere, in reality it exists only where it is being fought. Inasmuch as these daily concerns are the real field on which the masses most directly experience the ubiquitous repressiveness of capitalist social relations, it follows that it is also on the terrain of everyday life that the elementary forms of class consciousness develop or are repressed. Consequently, it is only after the battle against repression has been engaged on this "micro-social" level through the struggle of the masses for their subjective advantage in the sphere of everyday life (including the level of the concrete relations between people in their work, their leisure, their private life), that they will become aware of the larger, "macro-social" context and the objective processes which ultimately determine the character of everyday life. In short, while class contradiction remains fundamental, it expresses itself in actual class struggle indirectly, through struggles which owe their immediate impetus to the transformations taking place in the various modalities of everyday life and culture. Revolutionary struggle is thus diffuse as well as specifically directed. It is expressed throughout the various cultural spheres and institutional contexts, in specific conflicts and the manifold transformations of individuals rather than in a polar opposition of capital and labor. Under the circumstances, the struggle of the proletarians to liberate themselves effectively from class domination requires not only a collective assault on the power of capital but also a concept and practice of cultural revolution and psychological self-liberation.

Reich's essays of the early and middle 1930s[9]—including "The Sexual Struggle of Youth" and "What Is Class Consciousness?"—present what was perhaps the most successful attempt at a programmatic formulation aimed at such a unification of the struggles of the proletariat against the power and institutions of the ruling class with a cultural revolutionary project aimed at weakening the inhibiting influence of the authoritarian character structure of adults and forestalling its development in the young, thus facilitating the development "of people with a character structure which would make them capable of self-regulation." [10] Within the general framework of such a politics of everyday life, the struggle of the proletariat for workers' power within the context of the workplace remained a vital and fundamental element, and Reich, in formulating his concept of "work-democracy," was only reasserting the emphasis of a previous generation of revolutionary syndicalists and council communists on the struggle for workers' control as the most fundamental element of the whole revolutionary process, as both its form and its content, its principal means and its irreducible end.[11] According to this conception, the shaping of a "new man" free of authoritarian fixations does not take place either as a result of the ideological influence of socialist propaganda or as a mechanical side effect of the transformation of social relations as a whole, but rather involves "the development of a new psychic character in relation to [a struggle for] the democratic transformation of the *units of social production.*" [12] Thus, Reich argued:

> One of the social revolution's promises is that it will socialize the large factories, i.e., place them under the self-management of the workers. . . . Revolutionary work in factories can be successful only if it arouses the workers' *objective* interests in production and proceeds from there. But workers today have no interest in production as such, certainly not in the present form of production. In order to acquire a revolutionary interest in production they must think of it as their own property *now* under capitalism. . . . Our propaganda must make it clear that it is the workers, not the present owners of capital and the means of production, who are the real masters

of the factory. . . . [Otherwise] the average non-political or politically deformed industrial worker will react [to the attempt to expropriate the large capitalists] with a sense of guilt and a certain inhibition, as though he were seizing someone else's property. . . . [In contrast, once] he becomes conscious of his legitimate ownership, which is based on his labor; then the bourgeois view of the "sacred" nature of private property loses its power over [him]. . . . So workers in factories must start *now* to prepare for the takeover of these factories. They must learn to think for themselves, they must train themselves to look out for everything that will be needed and to think of how it should be organized. . . . Without any doubt this is the only way in which workers can be given an interest in the social revolution. . . . The actual takeover of power in the factories must be preceded by concrete preparation for this takeover *in the mind.*[13]

Despite its fundamental importance for the development of the workers' capacity for self-organization, to Reich, in contrast with the council communists and anarcho-syndicalists, the struggle for proletarian power within the workplace was a necessary and not a sufficient condition for the emergence of revolutionary consciousness. This was true because, as a result of the very development of the productive forces, there is a tendency for working time to be reduced and an increasing portion of the workers' activity to be taken up by problems of everyday life only indirectly related to production. And at the same time there is a parallel and related tendency for the individual's entry into production to be postponed and for the young increasingly to begin work with their character structure already highly developed and profoundly inhibited as regards their capacity to resist authoritarian manipulation. It follows that, as Agnes Heller and Milhály Vajda have recently reminded us: "Democracy at the level of production can become natural and free from manipulation, only if democratic life and norms of action have *already* become natural for the individual entering production." [14]

In other words, the struggle to weaken the inhibiting influences of character structure in adults through the constant encouragement of their social responsibility and capacity for self-organization is central, but what is even more important is the struggle to forestall the formation of an authoritarian character structure in the young, even *before* their entry into production, by an attack on the repressive institutions of the family, church, and school, which are not only the basic agencies by which the domination of the ruling class is first imposed on the individual's character structure but which also serve, through the manipulation of the fears, anxieties, and fixations thus created, to reinforce continually this internalized domination. Without this struggle against the fundamental authoritarian fixations inculcated by the family, the proletariat's struggle for power will prove illusory because its class enemy will, in a sense, remain hidden within its own self. In the terms of psychoanalysis, the values of the ruling class will continue to represent a sort of cultural ego ideal for the proletariat which, as a result, will remain fixed in a position of purely symmetrical opposition to it. The struggle to overcome the bourgeoisie thus represents both a personal and a historical mission—the equivalent for a whole social class of the process of personal maturation that Freud saw as commencing with the internalization of the parental ego ideal, or superego, and ending in symbolic patricide and a merging with the father's spirit. As Reich put it, depriving the ruling class of its power means, "at the same time, the elimination of the power of the father over the members of the family, and of the representation of the state *within* the compulsive family as the structure-forming cell of the class society." [15]

From this perspective we can understand the key role

assigned by Reich to the struggle of youth in the creation of a new cultural revolutionary movement—a movement which would incorporate sexual politics into revolutionary politics and unite an understanding of the conflicts arising out of everyday life with a broad political perspective aiming at the total transformation of society. Such a movement, Reich reasoned, would both provide the left with a weapon with which it might appropriately respond to political reaction's hitherto successful attempts to exploit the masses' suppressed sexual powers, and, conversely, offer a means of incorporating into the proletarian struggle the enormous untapped revolutionary potential represented by the contradiction between the requirements of human instincts and the constraints placed upon their satisfaction by the authoritarian institutions of patriarchal civilization. This contradiction is encountered first and in its most volatile form by youth within the family and accounts for the fact that during adolescence every human being finds him or herself compelled to carry out a personal campaign of more or less violent resistance to authority and to everything else that appears as a threat to the development of his or her own personality. Such resistance may have social and political significance, but only if the rebel's objective is not personal power—a share in the authority held by his or her elders—but rather personal emancipation, the abolition of authority. In the latter case, adolescent revolt may have implications that go beyond individual experience, for any overthrow of authority demonstrates that rulers are vulnerable and that submission is neither natural nor inevitable. Thus, for the young proletarian, as Reich wrote in "The Sexual Struggle of Youth," "the road which leads to the outbreak of class struggle passes by way of the struggle against the familial environment." [16] In order to move along this road from adolescent rebellion to anti-capitalist struggle, it is above all necessary that the natural tendencies of the young toward self-regulation be encouraged and defended against the traps of reactionary sexual politics and manipulation from above:

> Working-class youth will take part in concrete trade-union work. Others will concern themselves with organizing their personal lives, dealing with their parental conflicts, solving the problems of a sexual partner and housing. In this way they will create new forms of social life (at first only in the mind); then they will argue and eventually fight for these new forms; eventually nothing will stop them. Talks on the political situation or even about the "sexual problem of youth" are useless. That is control from above. Youth must begin *as from now* to organize its own life in every field. At first in doing this, it cannot pay much attention to the authorities or the police, nor should we expect it to; it should go right ahead and do what it thinks right and what it believes it can accomplish. It will realize soon enough that it is rigidly fenced in on all sides, that the system makes it impossible to organize even the simplest and most obvious things in the life of young people; thus their own practice will show them what is revolutionary politics and revolutionary necessity.[17]

At the same time, like the revolt of youth, the rebellion of women "against marriage as an economic bondage and a sexual restriction becomes a valuable asset of the revolutionary movement only if we supply objective and truthful expositions of these thorny problems." [18] More specifically:

> Experience teaches us that, for example, extra-marital sex or the desire for it is a factor which could prove extremely effective in the struggle against reactionary influences. But since it always goes hand in hand with a desire for security in marriage, we cannot develop it in the proper direction just by telling women that in the Soviet Union the distinction between marital and extra-marital sex has been abolished.[19]

This is also why, according to Reich, slogans affirming women's right to "integration into the production process," to "an end to dependence on men," or to "winning control over one's body," achieved relatively little by way of concrete advances for Soviet women. Even though

> the wish for economic independence, for independence from the male, and above all for sexual independence, are the most important components of the class-consciousness of women, . . . women's strong tendency toward bondage is reinforced by some characteristic fears: a fear of Soviet-style marriage legislation that would entail the loss of the husband as the provider; a fear of having no legally sanctioned sexual partner; and a fear of a free life in general.

These latter are "at least equally powerful inhibiting elements on the negative side." [20] Finally, "a fear that the proposed collective upbringing of children might 'take them away' from their mothers has acted as a powerful brake on clear political thinking." [21] In this regard,

> the principal question confronting the women's movement is undoubtedly that of the future of the family and the raising of children. In the Sex-Pol movement in Germany, we succeeded in winning over many women by explaining that socialism only proposes new forms for the communal life of men, women and children; and that the so-called abolition of the family under Bolshevism means no more than the separation of sexual interests from economic ones.[22]

Reich recognized that these efforts to complement the struggle for social revolution with a parallel movement for sexual emancipation that might serve to undermine the authoritarian tendencies in the average psychic structure of the masses were necessarily partial, limited by the fact that their full realization was ultimately "contingent on the control of the whole educational and ideological apparatus of the society," [23] and that this apparatus remained in the hands of the bourgeoisie. He nevertheless felt that there was much that could be accomplished toward this end through an intermediate program of "structural reforms," such as those outlined by the Sex-Pol movement in the early thirties. Among these demands were the following:

1. Better housing conditions for the masses of people.
2. Abolition of laws against abortion and homosexuality.
3. Change of marriage and divorce laws.
4. Free birth-control advice and contraceptives.
5. Health protection of mothers and children.
6. Nurseries in factories and other large employment centers.
7. Abolition of laws prohibiting sex education.
8. Home leave for prisoners.[24]

The struggle for these intermediate goals, while not involving the immediate realization of total sexual liberation for the masses, would at least hold out the possibility of partially relieving their needs and "forestalling the embourgeoisement of their sexual psychology," [25] which would leave them vulnerable to reactionary manipulation. More important, to Reich this struggle would give impetus to a process of coming-to-consciousness among the masses, necessarily "leading to the criticism of present-day society and to direct conflict with state authority." It was this *conflict*, he argued, which "was revolutionary, and not the all-too-limited degree of sexual liberation which is possible today." [26]

What is implicit in such a program of intermediate or transitional goals—of "revolutionary reforms," as André Gorz was to call them thirty years later[27]—is the attempt to develop a mode of struggle which will have as its objective not a peaceful transition to power but the crucial struggle on the ideological or cultural front, such as Gramsci called for. Through this struggle the masses will become prepared for the final clash with the bourgeoisie over state power, first by developing their subjective awareness of the actuality of an alternative to the existing mode of socioeconomic organization and, once they have grasped the necessity and possibility

of an alternative, by developing the capacity for self-organization within the proletariat which is essential to the carrying
out of this transformation. In contrast to Social Democratic
reformism or Leninist cadre organizations with their agit-
prop tactics, such a practice does not see "class consciousness
[as] something to be taught to the masses like lessons in
school—as a set of doctrines; rather, it is [seen as something]
to be elicited, drawn out of the masses' own experience [as]
the discovery of the politics of all human needs." [28]* Political
work is seen as necessarily going beyond mere propagandistic
criticism of existing society to take on a positive, construc-
tive, and anticipatory character as well—that is, to constitute
a coming-to-consciousness within different groups and strata
through a process of confronting concrete problems in the
interests of a struggle for the self-organization of one or
another aspect of their daily lives. Closely connected with
this conception of revolutionary consciousness and the
dynamics of mass politicization is a new approach to the
problems of revolutionary organization, founded on the
autonomy of the base rather than on "top-down" directives.
To be sure, this perspective does not reject the need for
leadership or for a revolutionary party: the revolution is still
seen as in need of coordination and direction, but what is
definitely rejected is any form of "substitutionism" of the

---

* More generally, Reich further clarifies the differences between the
politics of Sex-Pol and of Bolshevism or Social Democracy in the letter to
the Spanish anarchists (see n.23), in which he defines its general objectives
as the assimilation of the major precepts of anarchism into Marxism and
its specific objectives as including: "(a) the incorporation of sexual politics
into revolutionary politics; (b) the creation of a new attitude on the part of
the revolutionary leadership toward the masses (starting from their needs
and not 'top-down' directives); (c) the recognition of the cultural process as
a socially determined process of the transformation of sexual energy; (d)
the undertaking of theoretical and practical work regarding [the nature of]
the education appropriate to free men in a socialist society."

party as a subject of that revolutionary process which
articulates and administers for the masses what their own
structural immaturity prohibits them from formulating for
themselves.

This new notion of leadership is in the "Luxemburgist"
tradition in that it rejects narrow organizational solutions to
the problems of revolutionary struggle and emphasizes the
development of the masses' capacity for self-organization as
the basic aim of revolutionary struggle. In the original
Luxemburg formulation, however, there remains an unsolved
problem whose resolution becomes possible only in the light
of this new conception of the cultural revolutionary project.
This is the problem of how the party can perform the
necessary function of giving coherence to the fragmented
struggles of the proletariat ("socializing its consciousness")
without at the same time institutionalizing some form of
organizational hegemony over these struggles which would
eventually give rise to the growth of a revolutionary elite.
The Luxemburgist notion of organization is unable to
overcome the dilemma posed by the apparent inevitability of
the tendency toward the formation of oligarchies within all
large-scale organizations characterized by a division of labor
between leaders and masses, "thinkers" and "workers," etc.
Hence it can only perpetually oscillate between the antitheti-
cal imperatives constituted by the priority given to spontaneity, self-government, and the refusal of any delegation of
power, and the necessity for political direction, coordination,
and education.[29] In contrast, the cultural revolutionary
perspective—by virtue of its recognition of the cultural
process as a socially determined process for the transformation of surplus psychosexual energy—at least suggests the
possibility of establishing a dialectical relationship between
an avant-garde and the proletariat within which the oligarchi-
cal tendency for the leader-masses relation to become
institutionalized is checked by a countervailing process of

psychocultural emancipation aimed at the dissolution of the internalized compulsions within the psychic make-up of individuals that provide the affective underpinnings for the formation of the sort of dependent relationships with leaders and institutional elites that constitute the essential psychodynamics of the Michelian iron law of oligarchy. Thus, authority will only be allowed to exist in such a milieu inasmuch as it is truly rational—that is, inasmuch as it derives from the actual expertise of the leader vis-à-vis specific ends and conscious objectives determined by the masses themselves and corresponds to a real community of struggle and interest—and does not threaten to transform itself into an arrogated authority based on the masses' inability to comprehend their own interests rationally and their irrational infantile attachment to charismatic figures and leadership cliques. Such an organization would be based, in short, on the incorporation of sexual politics into revolutionary politics. In contrast to the traditional Marxist party structure, which has oscillated between a monolithic discipline of an authoritarian type and the struggle of factions through the manipulation of assemblies, groups, and sections, it would constitute a truly human milieu, a counter-community providing the broadest possible range of communication and collective experience and a prefiguration of the free society it wants to realize.

Notes

1. Heller and Vajda, "Family Structure and Communism," p. 102.
2. Gerald Gill, "Armed Insurrection," *Arena*, no. 27 (1971), p. 9.
3. Ibid.
4. Max Horkheimer, "Die Philosophie der absoluten Konzentration," *Zeitschrift für Sozialforschung*, vol. 7 (1938), p. 300.

5. Michael Schneider, "Vanguard, Vanguard, Who's Got the Vanguard?", Part I, *Liberation*, vol. 17, no. 2 (May 1972), p. 28.

6. Horkheimer, "Die Juden und Europa."

7. Wilhelm Reich, "On Revolutionary Organization" (1934), *Liberation*, vol. 17, no. 1 (April 1972), p. 23.

8. Horkheimer, *Authoritärer Staat* (Amsterdam, 1968), p. 68.

9. An English translation of the most important of these is in Lee Baxandall's collection of Reich's political writings, *Wilhelm Reich, Sex-Pol Essays: 1929–1934* (New York, 1972). Further writings by Reich and his comrades in the Sex-Pol movement are reprinted from his journal, *Zeitschrift für politische Psychologie und Sexual-ökonomie*, in Hans-Peter Gente, ed., *Marxismus, Psychoanalyse, Sexpol*, vol. I (Frankfurt, 1971).

10. Reich, *The Sexual Revolution*, p. 26.

11. Among the most important statements of the "council communist" position are: Herman Gorter, *Réponse à Lénine* (1920; Paris, 1960); Anton Pannekoek, *Workers' Councils* (Melbourne, 1947); Antonio Gramsci, "The Soviets in Italy" (1919), *New Left Review*, no. 51 (September–October 1968), pp. 25–58. More recently, this perspective found perhaps its most important post-World War II voice in the French journal *Socialisme ou Barbarie*.

12. Heller and Vajda, "Family Structure," p. 105.

13. Reich, "What Is Class Consciousness?", pp. 48–49.

14. Heller and Vajda, "Family Structure," p. 106.

15. Reich, *The Sexual Revolution*, p. 106.

16. Reich, *La lutte sexuelle des jeunes*, p. 124.

17. Reich, "What Is Class Consciousness?", p. 49.

18. Ibid., p. 28.

19. Ibid.

20. Ibid.

21. Ibid.

22. Ibid., p. 29. For an account of an actual attempt to institute a communal form of child-raising along "Reichian" lines, carried out quite recently by members of the German student movement, see the article on "Kommune 2: A Radical

Approach to Family and Child-Rearing," *Liberation*, vol. 17, no. 8 (January 1973).

23. Reich, "Antwort auf einige Einwände der Anarchisten Genossen," *Zeitschrift für politische Psychologie und Sexual-ökonomie*, vol. 3 (1936), p. 47. This note, written in reply to a group of Spanish anarchists, while published under the name of Karl Teschitz, is attributed to Reich by Sinelnikoff, *L'oeuvre de Wilhelm Reich*, vol. II, p. 113.

24. See Ilse Olmendorf Reich, *Wilhelm Reich: A Personal Biography* (New York, 1969), pp. 21–22.

25. Reich, "Antwort auf einige Einwände der Anarchisten Genossen," p. 48.

26. Ibid., p. 49.

27. See André Gorz, *Strategy for Labor* (Boston, 1967) and his essay "Reform and Revolution," in *The Socialist Register 1968* (New York, 1968), pp. 111–44.

28. Reich, "On Revolutionary Organization," p. 22.

29. The implicit presence of this problematic within the Luxemburgist approach is particularly well illustrated by the recent debates between Luxemburgians and Maoists within the Italian ultra-left. See, for example, the debate between Adriano Sofri and Romano Luperini, "Quelle avant-garde? Quelle organisation?", *Les temps modernes*, no. 279 (October 1969), pp. 435–54.

6

From Crisis Capitalism to a Bureaucratic Society of Manipulated Consumption

Although the Sex-Pol movement was ultimately unsuccessful in its bid to introduce a new cultural revolutionary dimension to the struggles of the left in the 1930s, its importance should nevertheless be obvious today, when a revolutionary New Left is once again opening up the question of personal liberation and its relation to the broader social revolution. For it is to the undying credit of the early cultural revolutionaries to have first posed these problems. Above all, they opened up the whole problem of the political significance of sexual repression and of the manner in which social domination becomes internalized in the personality, and revealed the great untapped revolutionary potential represented by the struggles of youth and women. Despite all this, it would be naive and politically regressive to assume that the movement today can simply pick up where Reich or the Surrealists left off, or that the Reichian strategy enunciated in "What Is Class Consciousness?" provides in itself a strategic and programmatic basis capable of overcoming the crippling disjunction between sociopolitical revolution and personal emancipation now confronting the New Left. Perspectives which may have been adequate to the circumstances under which the class struggle was being waged in the 1930s, and which may even form an indispensable point of

148

departure for future theoretical advances, do not constitute a sufficient intellectual basis for the resumption of revolutionary struggle. Neither do they permit us to dispense with the obligation of all revolutionaries to keep abreast of reality by the continual up-dating and modification of old categories and/or the introduction of new ones in the light of actual historical development.

Underlying this need for a constant up-dating of revolutionary theory and practice is the fact that we are currently undergoing one of the most extraordinary and massive processes of transformation in the whole history of humanity —more profound and disruptive even than those of such periods as the Renaissance or the first Industrial Revolution. Driven forward by the scientific and technical revolution of this century and by the simultaneous unfication of the world, this transformation is giving birth to a totally new civilization, new in regard to its ecological environment as much as to its technical-economic base, its social structure, its mental superstructure, its means of communication, and its modes of perception. Only its chief attributes and contradictory consequences need be mentioned here. They include: the impact of automation and cybernation, which transform both the relations between worker and machine and the whole nature of administration and knowledge production; the explosive growth of cities and the urbanization of the countryside; the near disappearance of the peasant or independent farmer class in the industrial countries and, at the same time, the radicalization of the peasantry in the Third World. Simultaneous with these processes, which accompany the transition from competitive or "crisis" capitalism into organized or state capitalism, there is a second revolution taking place in the sphere of everyday life. Among the characteristics of this second great transformation of our era are the dissolution of the patriarchal family, the partial emancipation of youth and women, the liberation of sexuality, and the creation of new opportunities for increased leisure, consumption, and education on the part of the proletarian masses.

Reich, standing at the threshold of this vast transformation, recognized that it involved a "deep-reaching revolution of our cultural living," which, while proceeding "without parades, uniforms, drums, or cannon salutes," nonetheless was claiming as its victims "no fewer than those [revolutions] of 1848 or 1917," for it "goes to the roots of our emotional, social, and economic existence." [1] It was on the basis of his insight into these processes that Reich directed his efforts toward a reformulation of the revolutionary project, incorporating the goals of sexual liberation and cultural revolution. As a consequence he was able, as we have argued, to develop a perspective which was uniquely appropriate to the conditions under which the class struggle was being waged in the interwar years. Had this perspective been able to overcome the intransigence and immobilism of the institutionalized proletarian movement, it might have pointed the way to proletarian revolution instead of fascist reaction in the West. The fact that it failed, and the subsequent further development of society in the period following World War II in directions Reich could not have anticipated, have necessitated new theoretical and practical efforts.

As the initial period of illusory optimism which followed the defeat of fascism was giving way to the realization that the overthrow of fascism had not brought into being a new, life-oriented climate in the advanced industrial world, it was also becoming increasingly clear that the unprecedented development of science and technology which was taking place during this period not only portended dramatic new possibilities for human emancipation from the burdens of toil and scarcity, but also harbored previously unrecognized means for perpetuating domination and repression. The vast expansion of scientific specialization engaged, directly or indirectly, in production was accompanied by the increasing application of technical knowledge to the sphere of social organization and by the growth of a techno-bureaucratic mentality in place of the old liberal perspective. Through an ever greater fetishization of power, conformism, and alienation, "the powers that had defeated fascism by virtue of their technical and economic superiority" would, as Marcuse put it, "strengthen and streamline the social structure which had produced fascism." [2] The subsequent establishment of a dehumanized consumer society with its manipulative mass media and all-pervasive bureaucratic apparatus appeared not only to have permitted the bourgeoisie throughout the West to maintain its hegemony—restoring the world of bourgeois everyday life wherever it had been disrupted, strengthening it elsewhere—but also to have increasingly facilitated the integration within a manipulative consensus of even those very social forces—the industrial proletariat in particular—which had hitherto been seen as the principal agencies of anti-capitalist struggle within an evolving capitalist system. Nor were the industrial workers alone in their acquiescence: women, for instance, who had struggled for equal rights during the 1920s and 1930s and who, under wartime conditions, especially in the United States, had finally made an impressive entrance into economic and intellectual life, now returned to their old roles as housewives and mothers within their new suburban ghettos. The oppressed masses in the West were increasingly acquiescing in a more and more manipulative system of domination which, instead of offering a transcendence of their alienation and exploitation, simply promised ever higher levels of material compensation for it in the form of a rising level of individual consumption; at the same time, the construction of socialism in the East was proceeding under conditions of forced industrial accumulation and increasing bureaucratization which could only further serve to discredit the Marxist project.

To be sure, this reorganization and stabilization of the advanced industrial societies in the postwar era in no way eliminated the objective contradictions of the capitalist system; on the contrary, they were more intense than ever before. It did, however, reflect a new development in the system's capacity to suppress or attenuate the traditional and explosive forms in which these contradictions had previously expressed themselves and, above all, to stifle the development of a subjective awareness of the liberating potentialities latent in the development of the productive forces of late capitalism. Postwar capitalism responded to the objective growth of its basic contradictions and to the potentially explosive social forces set in motion by this aggravation with an ever more efficient repressive mobilization of all the system's resources. In particular, the new role of knowledge and technique in production was extended to the functions of power as well, resulting in the gradual obliteration of the functional difference between base and superstructure.[3] As a consequence, the ruling class succeeded in fusing political, administrative, and economic processes within a single overarching apparatus of control and in imposing its institutionalized domination over all aspects of everyday life. Work, leisure, education, consumption, personal relations, even sexuality, became integrated within the repressive logic of the whole, and all the conflicts which arose within these spheres were in turn reduced to the status of technical problems to be dealt with by administrative measures. The need for a new "legitimation" of power—a need created by the collapse of the self-regulating market economy of lassez-faire capitalism and by the failure of fascist irrationalism effectively to replace liberal ideology as a rationalization of class domination—led increasingly toward a technocratic ideology of "substitute programming" as a principal ideological justification for the continued power of the capitalist class. Throughout the advanced capitalist world we can discern the emergence of a new capitalist society, a *bureau-cratic society of manipulated consumption** characterized by an increasingly complete interpenetration between politi-cal and economic power, along with an attempt to institu-tionalize the class struggle through the increasing bureaucrat-ization, co-optation, and integration of potential forces of opposition.

Within this bureaucratic society of controlled consump-tion, the fun and games of repressive affluence, in which the individual participates at the point of consumption, have as their admission price the continuing surrender of control over increasing areas of his/her life to the quasi-totalitarian apparatus. As a consequence of this progressive disappear-ance of all remaining areas of choice or autonomy, there is a dual loss: in the private sphere, the loss of a sense of personal identity; in the public sphere, the loss of any meaningful political life. Even the autonomy of organizations originating in an earlier era of class struggle and formally dedicated to the defense of the interests of the oppressed against the ruling class and the state becomes illusory in the face of the current extension of the system's administrative apparatus.

The emergence of this manipulative process of substitut-ing the impersonal goals and aims of society for the individual's own processes of selection in order to produce a coincidence between individual and social needs is, of course, rooted in the need for late capitalism to preserve need, scarcity, inequality, and oppression in the face of a develop-

---

* I have borrowed the term from Lefebvre, for whom it is superior to other terms inasmuch as it defines both "this society's rational character . . . as well as the limits set to its rationality (bureaucratic); [both] the object of its organization (consumption instead of production) and the *level* at which it operates and upon which it is based (everyday life)." More generally, he argues "this definition has the advantage of being *scientific* and more *precisely* formulated than others [such as state monopoly capitalism]." [4]

ment of the productive forces which renders all of these obsolete. As the development of these forces generates an increasing social surplus, it becomes increasingly necessary for the logic of commodity relations to penetrate more and more areas of social life. The corporate apparatus has to create false needs, open new markets, and colonize ever more of society, not because of any shortage of productive capacity or technical knowledge, but because there is no longer any "natural" drive to expand this capacity. With the increasing tendency toward the elimination of the "natural" basis of scarcity, with the creation of surpluses in every area—surplus goods, surplus manpower, surplus capital, surplus knowledge, etc.—it has become increasingly necessary to condition capitalist expansion through the artificial creation of appropriate new forms of need and scarcity: scarcity of jobs, scarcity of collective facilities, scarcity of leisure, lack of security and freedom, etc.[5]

Insofar as this reorganization of economic production and reproduction under late capitalism requires the increasing replacement of production for use by waste production, the increasing obsolescence of old techniques and commodities along with the creation of ever greater numbers of new products, and the penetration of ever larger spheres of life by the commodity market, it also must increasingly develop new techniques for ensuring the compliance of the masses with these new imperatives. In contrast to competitive capitalism's reliance on the restriction of consumption as a principal means of enforcing social discipline, late capitalism must virtually compel individuals to consume whatever and whenever is dictated by the need to absorb the system's rising economic surplus. Moreover, since these forms of consumption, and the work people are constrained to perform in order to partake of them, become increasingly irrational, the relationship between the sphere of production and the other spheres of life must be removed from the scrutiny or perception of individuals. Purely economic sanctions partially lose their efficacy as a means of disciplining the working population due to the new level of material abundance made possible by the technical and scientific revolution, the growth of an increasingly well-educated work force, and the process of the collectivization of life through urbanization, as well as to the disintegration of old superstructures and traditional symbols of legitimation. The older forms of class domination, while by no means eliminated, are increasingly supplemented as the main support for class power by new forms of institutional domination over all aspects of daily life and by the increasingly effective instruments thus created for the manipulation of behavior and consciousness:

[It is] not that manipulation has replaced and cancelled out exploitation. But it becomes evident, when one observes the manipulation of needs, and of situations producing pseudo-satisfaction in the commodity market, in communications, and in sexuality, that exploitation is not now confined to its direct physical form but relies upon a gigantic apparatus of created needs which are constantly being manipulated to get people to comply with meaningless social goals. Even the structure of exploitation has changed. The classic structure was: minimization both of primary needs (food, clothing, sexuality) and of secondary needs (free time, sport, etc.), with, *in contrast*, maximization of exploitation (low pay, long working hours, accelerated work tempo, women and children at work, very few social benefits or none at all). The present structure is: manipulative optimization of needs which accord with the needs of the system, abolition of the difference between primary and secondary needs, and *thereby* maximization of exploitation.[6]

This transformation of the mechanisms of economic production and reproduction, and of the nature and extent of class hegemony, has necessarily been accompanied by an equally pervasive modification of the system's psychic environment. The very same process of "internal colonization" by which the neocapitalist apparatus has extended itself throughout society via the creation and satisfaction of profitable needs—a process which has itself become an essential component of the system of domination—has had profound consequences both for the psychic development of individuals and for the nature of the society made up of such individuals. Adorno put it well when he remarked that "this regimentation, the result of the progressive societalization of all human relations, did not simply confront the mind from without; it immigrated into its immanent consistency." [7] As a result of the increasingly universal extension of the world of commodity relations and of hierarchical power, there has been a corresponding subversion of those old ways of forming character which were the object of psychoanalytic investigation, and the substitution of new ones:

> (1) First, the classical psychoanalytic model, in which the father and the father-dominated family was the agent of mental socialization, is being invalidated by society's direct management of the nascent ego through the mass media, school and sport teams, gangs, etc. (2) Second, this decline in the role of the father follows the decline of the role of private and family enterprise; the son is increasingly less dependent on the father and the family tradition in selecting and finding a job and in earning a living. The socially necessary repressions and the socially necessary behavior are no longer learned— and internalized—in the long struggle with the father—the ego ideal is rather brought to bear on the ego directly and "from outside," *before* the ego is actually formed as the personal and (relatively) autonomous subject of mediation between him-*self* and others.[8]

Reich had looked forward to such a disintegration of patriarchal authority and the compulsive family's socializing functions, but this, according to Marcuse, was because he saw only the liberating potential of this process and failed to

anticipate the contradictory consequences such a development would have under the present conditions of the
repressive organization of every aspect of everyday life by
hierarchical power and its overarching apparatus of manipulation and control. He failed to grasp the manner in which
such a partial liberation of the child from family-imposed
constraints on her or his development would be rendered
meaningless by the immediate transference of these familial
functions to extra-familial agencies and the child's subsequent subjection, through these agencies, to an even more
rigorous process of repressive socialization. According to
Marcuse and the Frankfurt Marxists, Reich did not anticipate these developments in part because, in his emphasis on
the role of the classical compulsive family form as "a factory
for the reproduction of authoritarian personalities," he
overlooked the extent to which, submerged beneath its more
obvious repressive functions, it also contained certain anti-
authoritarian possibilities. The family, as an independent
and (relatively) isolated unit, at least provided the possibility
of a more or less protected "space" in which the individual
could develop his or her ego *against* the external society—
that is, it supplied an intellectual and sometimes a physical
refuge which made resistance possible. Thus, although within
this space familial relations partook of the prevailing inhumanity, they also preserved at least the possibility of
something more human.[9] Inasmuch as, to quote Horkheimer, "within the family, unlike public life, relationships
were not mediated through the market and the individual
members were not competing with each other, the individual
always had the possibility there of living not as a mere
function but as a human being." [10]

The elimination of this vital "free space" for individual
self-development has meant that these changes in the process
and agencies of socialization have undermined the autonomy
of the ego and constitute the psychological basis for what

Marcuse calls the "formation of *masses*"—a process through which the mediation between the Self and the Other gives way to immediate identification. The consequences of this process are twofold: "In the social structure, the individual becomes the conscious and unconscious object of administration and obtains his freedom and satisfaction in his role *as* such an object; in the mental structure, the ego shrinks to such an extent that it seems no longer capable of sustaining itself, as a self, in distinction from id and superego." [11] In short, the individual loses the capacity for a multi-dimensional development, such as had been the aim of psychoanalysis, which would maintain a balance between autonomy and heteronomy, freedom and unfreedom, pleasure and pain; she or he is rendered one dimensional through the infusion of the content of her/his ego from the outside by the apparatus of social domination. "Having control of the apparatus," Marcuse argues, "means having control of the masses in such a way, in fact, that this control seems to result automatically from the division of labor, to be its technical result, the rationale of the functioning apparatus that spans and maintains the whole society." [12] A "technical code" replaces the old moral code, and "domination appears as a technical-administrative quality" [13]—an expression of objective reason.

Given the success of the apparatus of total administration in this production of "masses," whereby every facet of technical development is redirected toward the maximum passive isolation of the individual, toward his/her total control through a direct, permanent, and one-way transmission of directives from above, it has been possible for the system to overcome the disjunctions between the rising levels of individual consumption and waste production required for the absorption of the economic surplus, and the libidinal structures of the anal-obsessive character with its propensities toward thrift, deferred gratification, anti-sexuality, etc. In order to ensure that individuals consume whatever and whenever the needs of the economic system dictate, the classical anal character has been relaxed in favor of a "looser" structure characterized by a desire for instant gratification, by the predominance of emotions over consciousness and conscience.*

This transformation, involving a new "pre-formation" of the personality and its development down to the deepest instinctual level in the interests of the dominant socioeconomic system, is seen by Marcuse as corresponding to an "administered" relaxation of restrictions on the satisfaction of libidinal impulses on a scale Reich would have regarded as incompatible with the maintenance of class domination. It is in regard to this phenomenon that Marcuse has introduced the notion of a "controlled" or "repressive" desublimation through which the release of restraints on the real and apparent libidinal gratifications afforded by the system's new productive capacity not only serves to enhance the ideologi-

---

* See Reimut Reiche's *Sexuality and Class Struggle*. It should, however, be noted that while a central thesis of Reiche's book is "that the ever present problems of overproduction make it necessary to relax the classical anal obsessional character," in contrast to some psychoanalytically inspired investigators of advanced industrial society (such as Mitscherlich who, in his *Society Without the Father*, speaks of the spread of a new "oral, demanding" character), Reiche insists that this "relaxation" of the anal character does not mean that it has disappeared altogether. Although in the sphere of consumption there is indeed a tendency toward "oral" models of behavior characterized by a sort of "perpetual puberty"; in the realm of production, in contrast, "what counts, with only a few exceptions, are the old 'anal' laws of order, thrift and rigid sexual morality." As a result of the existence of such contrary models of behavior in the respective spheres of production and consumption, it follows for Reiche that something like a collective tendency toward ego-division arises: "individuals must cultivate two contradictory character traits, and daily demonstrate the corresponding modes of behavior—rigidity, classic authoritarianism and anti-sexuality at work; 'relaxation,' objectless festishisms and 'apparent' sexuality in free time." [14]

cal legitimacy of the system, but is also channeled into forms functional to the system's need to increase consumption.[15] For Marcuse, repressive desublimation extends liberty while intensifying domination. Whereas in former societies, restrictions on sexual gratification were necessary for the survival of civilization—since conditions of scarcity demanded the perpetual toil of the majority—today, "in contrast, the advanced industrial society democratizes release from repression—a compensation which serves to strengthen the government which allows it, and the institutions which administer the compensation." [16] Thus, while the opportunities for sexual freedom are extended, at the same time this desublimation is directed into prescribed institutional channels, and one of the effects is to restrict the release of sexuality to modes and forms which reduce and weaken erotic energy. Sexuality, isolated from those broader erotic components which provide the basis for a civilized human relationship, can be integrated into commerce and industry, entertainment and advertising, politics and propaganda. "To the degree to which sexuality obtains a definite sales value or becomes a token of prestige and of playing according to the rules of the game," Marcuse concludes, "it is itself transformed into an instrument of social cohesion." [17] Inasmuch as it provides a necessary form of release and compensation for individuals who are unable to utilize their own creative faculties in work and leisure time,

> repressive desublimation accompanies the contemporary tendencies towards the introjection of totalitarianism into the daily business and leisure of man, into his toil and into his happiness. It manifests itself in all the manifold ways of fun, relaxation, and togetherness which practice the destruction of privacy, the contempt of form, the inability to tolerate silence, the proud exhibition of crudeness and brutality.[18]

As a result of the system's success in mobilizing and

administering the release of libidinal energy through a process of controlled desublimation, it is necessary to reevaluate two basic premises of Reich's analysis and strategy. First of all, it seems increasingly difficult to accept the economic, physiological, and utopian functions which Reich ascribed to the liberation of genital sexuality within his conception of how general human emancipation was to be achieved: "While it was possible for Wilhelm Reich in his day to link every demand for the liberation of sexuality from the complex of forces oppressing it under the capitalist system, with a political demand which struck explicitly at the economic roots of the system," today, with the whole sphere of sexuality biased toward the system, "it has become very much more difficult to make the qualitative distinction between apparent and real sexual freedom." [19] In the second place, the same processes which have resulted in the partial integration of sexuality within the repressive society also cast doubt upon Reich's expectation that the strengthening of sexuality and the partial gratification of libidinal urges would involve a weakening of aggressiveness. Herbert Marcuse has criticized Reich's "undifferentiated" notion of sexual liberation for neglecting "the historical dynamic of the sex instincts and of their fusion with the destructive impulses." [20] * According to Marcuse, in light of the contempo-

---

* In a more recent work, *Counter-Revolution and Revolt*, Marcuse has clarified this criticism of Reich's political perspective. While "Reich was right in emphasizing the roots of fascism in instinctual repression," he argues, "he was wrong when he saw the mainsprings for the defeat of fascism in sexual liberation." For under conditions of advanced capitalism, "the latter can proceed quite far without endangering the . . . system." Furthermore, once this stage of development is reached and the "submissiveness, aggression, and the identification of the people with their leaders" comes to have "a rational rather than an instinctual basis," this also becomes a basis for the organization of hatred and aggression against those rebels who seek instinctual liberation. It follows that "instinctual libera-

rary phenomena of repressive and controlled desublimation it becomes necessary to consider "the possibility of a simultaneous release of repressed sexuality *and* aggressiveness." [22] Organized capitalism sublimates this frustration and primary aggressiveness on an unprecedented scale and, through the identification of individuals with their own aggressive goals, attempts to mobilize the population physically and mentally against the eventuality of its own supercession. It does this first of all by the creation of an enemy "against whom the aggressive energy which cannot be channeled into the normal, daily struggle for existence can be released." [23] This institutionalized enemy (for instance, the "Communist menace") is not simply an external threat, but represents the system's own suppressed potential as well. In mobilizing to meet this threat, through the stepped-up production of goods and services which do not enlarge individual consumption but rather constitute wasteful and destructive consumption (e.g., the military-industrial complex, the arms and space race, etc.), the system also mobilizes against its own obsolescence as a mode of production and of the exploitation of labor. On the private level as well as on the level of the nation as a whole, "destructive energy becomes socially useful aggressive energy and the aggressive behavior impels growth—growth of economic, political and technical power." [24] To be sure, frustration, unhappiness, and sickness· remain the basis of this sublimation, but the productivity and the brute power of the system serve to increase the capacity of the system to contain this resentment: "To the degree to which the society in its very structure becomes aggressive, the mental structure of its citizens adjusts itself: the individual becomes at one and the

---

tion becomes a force of social liberation only to the degree to which sexual energy is transformed into erotic energy, striving to change the mode of life on a social, political scale." [21]

same time more aggressive and more pliable and submissive, for he submits to a society which, by virtue of its affluence and power, satisfies his deepest (and otherwise greatly repressed) instinctual needs." [25]

The mental structure of the individual comes to reflect the contradictions which characterize the social structure of advanced capitalism. Within this society, the contradiction between the need to preserve the established system of power and privilege and the historical obsolescence of this need has required the increasing "transfer of power from the human individual to the technical or bureaucratic apparatus, from living to dead labor, from personal to remote control, from a machine (or group of machines) to a whole mechanized system." [26] As a result of this transfer of power, there also takes place a transfer of guilt feeling, responsibility: "It releases the individual from being an autonomous person— in work and in leisure, in his needs and satisfactions, in his thought and emotions." [27] At the same time, this release is not accompanied by a release from alienated labor: "The individuals must go on spending physical and mental energy in the struggle for existence, status, advantage; they must suffer, service, and enjoy the apparatus which imposes on them this necessity." Alienation is intensified even as it becomes ever more transparently anachronistic, yet to the extent that the society succeeds in providing a rising standard of material consumption, this consciousness of alienation is repressed as "individuals identify themselves with their being-for-others." [28] Inasmuch as individuals remain libidinally attached to the goods and services, to the pseudo-satisfactions which the system provides, they do not actualize their frustrations through opposition to the society itself. Within such a system,

> direct interpersonal experience is not possible; life becomes reduced to a show in the interests of the profit motive, a

display of commodities. This does not mean that experience becomes vicarious but that it becomes an act of self-consumption. Advertising makes the image a conscious fantasy, and we are consciously living it out in our daily lives. We enter the environment as consumers, and the environment of which we are part becomes the ultimate commodity. Since pseudo-experience is not gratifying as experience, we find our pleasure in its pseudo-ness—in the process of image-making, of technological manipulation. This is why contemporary advertising no longer directly glorifies the product but rather glorifies the system—the corporate image and finally advertising itself.[29]

Just as the transition from liberal capitalism to organized capitalism has seen the replacement of the self-regulatng marketplace in which a multitude of individual producers competed, so, in a similar development on the level of consumption, the isolated, individual commodity is subsumed within what Henri Lefebvre and the Situationists call the "spectacle" [30]—a process of manipulated consumption which complements the integration and concentration of production within giant corporate structures by fusing together all the individual acts of consumption into "spectacular" life-styles. In this way, late capitalism not only seeks, through its control of the mass media, to disguise the obsolescence of capitalist social relations and the material possibilities for liberation contained within them by creating the appearance of continual innovation through the presentation of a never ending series of spectacles, pseudo-dramas, fads, diversions, and even pseudo-rebellions disseminated by the mass media, but also to replace the traditional cultural systems of taboos, substitute gratifications, and symbols of legitimation, which once justified institutional power and which have collapsed as a result of late capitalist development, by a systematic organization of appearances which translates all the institutional rituals, patterns, and compromises in which social conflicts were previously stabilized into new relations of signs and objects. Elements of traditional bourgeois and popular culture, for instance, are converted into raw materials out of which the culture industry creates profitable new fads and fashions. The processes of spectacular consumption convert the most commonplace objects of everyday activity into stage props for this universal festival in which the fetishistic nature of commodities triumphs completely over their use-value. Thus, mass consumption goods and store windows, traffic and advertising, department stores and boutiques, sports and politics, architecture and media production, news and packaging, "come together to form a totality, a permanent theater, which dominates not only the public city centers but also private interiors." [31] As the ethos and mode of the spectacle come increasingly to penetrate the whole of culture, the processes of spectacular consumption carry to their logical conclusion the technological usurpation of imagination and of the unconscious—the replacement of real experience by pseudo-experience and of real communication by the one-way dissemination of directives and symbols from above—begun by the processes of repressive desublimation. Within this bureaucratized society and its culture of the spectacle, not only are women and men denied the possibility of comprehending the social whole or of integrating their experiences within a coherent framework which might give them meaning, but they also suffer from new repressions imposed on their libidinal and instinctual drives, and from a blockage of their imaginations, a blockage which seems to have a deforming effect on their primordial human functioning while making a new humanization of culture appear impossible since the whole dimension of transcendence has been extirpated from this culture.

Given the success of this counter-revolutionary mobilization of society's repressive forces—extending even to an administered relaxation of libidinal renunciations and to the replacement of traditional culture with a "spectacular" organization of everyday life aimed at promoting a false consciousness immunized against its own falsehood—it is no longer possible to share the overly optimistic perspectives of earlier cultural revolutionary movements like Sex-Pol or the Surrealists regarding the immediate prospects for a process of total human emancipation uniting social revolution with psychological, sexual, and aesthetic liberation. At the same time, the extreme pessimism of Marcuse's vision of a totally one-dimensional system which has foreclosed on all possibilities for emancipatory praxis is equally in error. Aiming at stability, consolidation, at preserving its own survival, at integrating the working class and smothering its traditional class antagonism, this society partially succeeds in achieving these goals (by the repressive organization of everyday life, by compulsion, by its ideology of consumerism more than by the reality of the consumption it affords), but only at the cost of maximizing repression. Inasmuch as the consensus which undeniably surrounds late capitalist society is not the spontaneous product of an organization of social life which has eliminated all real causes of conflict, but is rather the result of the imposition on that society of a gigantic apparatus of repression which stifles all attempts at human expression and communication, then it remains a society torn by contradictions. While these contradictions may not find immediate expression in mass struggles, they could, under the right circumstances, provide the basis for a new coming-to-consciousness among these masses.[32]

The growth of this system's contradictions can be perceived even on the economic level, despite the presence of instruments for stabilizing the economy and promoting economic growth. With the technological developments characteristic of late capitalism, the labor-displacing effect of progressive automation can only be offset by the ever greater absorption of surplus labor into parasitical jobs and services relating to the production of waste and means of destruction. At the same time, the accelerating burden of unproductive expenditures, combined with the costs of neocolonial wars, serve to deprive the system of the resources necessary to alleviate the disruptions of the social environment created by economic growth. A disjunction appears between the priorities of economic growth and those of social development, giving the familiar late-capitalist syndrome of poverty amidst affluence, of increasing individual consumption in the midst of a collapse of public services and a disintegration of the urban environment.[33] Tensions within the society are exacerbated by these ever more blatant contradictions between the vast social wealth produced under late capitalism and the wasteful and destructive uses of this wealth, between the priorities of capitalist accumulation and social needs, between the emancipatory potential of the productive forces and the actuality of repression, between the possible abolition of alienated labor and its preservation by the existing social relations. At the same time, these contradictory tendencies reveal the existence of limits to the capacity of this over-organized society and its spectacle indefinitely to repress a consciousness of these contradictions and of the creative power lurking beneath the misery and poverty of everyday life. Indeed, "the very intensity of the process of management and manipulation, the necessity for constant supervision in the realm of consciousness" within the system "is the best evidence of the essential fragility of the social structure which requires it." [34] The swindle which the "festivals" characterizing the processes of spectacular consumption perpetuates, while remaining a swindle, could also be the harbinger of something else:

> Consumption as spectacle contains the promise that want will disappear. The deceptive, brutal and obscene features of this festival derive from the fact that there can be no question

of a real fulfillment of its promise. But so long as scarcity holds sway, use-value remains a decisive category which can be abolished only by trickery. Yet trickery on such a scale is only conceivable if it is based on mass need. This need—it is a utopian one—is there. It is a desire for a new ecology, for a breaking-down of environmental barriers, for an aesthetic which is not limited to the sphere of the "artistic." These desires are not—or are not primarily—internalized rules of the game as played by the capitalist system. They have physiological roots and can no longer be suppressed. Consumption as spectacle is—in parody form—the anticipation of a Utopian situation.[35]

The same ambivalence can be seen in other areas as well. The promises of the media, for instance, may be considered responses to the mass need for nonmaterial variety and mobility, a need which the repressive system exploits through fetishistic forms such as private car ownership and tourism. Nevertheless, even though it may be set to music and orchestrated by the spectacle, loneliness persists and contrasts ever more painfully with the multiplication of messages, information, news, etc. There is, similarly, "a striking contrast between the incredible performances—at social and technical cost—to save a sick child, a wounded man, to prolong the agony of the dying; and the genocides, the conditions in our hospitals and of medicine in general, the difficulties encountered in obtaining remedies." [36] As satisfaction and dissatisfaction go hand in hand, contradiction—while not always on the surface—is implicit everywhere and may become explicit at almost any time with the articulation of immanent desires which, while capital tries to absorb them and rob them of their explosive force, nonetheless remain powerful and unequivocally emancipatory. Typically, these desires involve the need to participate in the social process on a local, national, and international level; the need for new forms of human interaction; the need for release from ignorance and tutelage; the need for self-determination.[37]

There is an inherent instability in the bureaucratic society of manipulated consumption, and this stability must inevitably increase as a consequence of such a society's innate incapacity to satisfy, within the existing social forms, any of the very needs on which it depends for its reproduction and which, through the mechanisms of spectacular consumption, it continually intensifies. Since the products and illusory satisfactions it provides cannot under any circumstances really satisfy the expectations they create, frustrations and unfulfilled desires accumulate into a fund of repressed resentment. As a result, just as this society appears to realize its goals—just as integration tends to become complete, incorporating all the old oppositional forms into the apparatus—it also tends to explode: "By fragmenting and multiplying the vexations, it thus arrives sooner or later at an atom of unlivable reality, and suddenly frees a nuclear energy that had become lost from sight beneath so much passivity and dreary resignation." [38] The image of total social integration collapses. As student opposition arises and, to quote Andrew Feenberg, "shows the individuals the way to a discharge of aggression on its real source, the 'system,'" [39] opposition in general once more becomes possible and thus necessary. New forms of struggle and contestation are invented and a new left arises on the basis of an immanent critique of the repressive society in terms of the unfulfilled promises upon which it rests, the needs to which it gives rise and then frustrates. This defines in turn a new project of cultural revolution through which the utopian content of these needs is given real content. Finally, with the attempt to actualize this project through the struggles of students, blacks and other minorities, and the women's movement, a qualitatively different kind of challenge is beginning to break through the stultifying embrace in which the system and its repressive consensus had contained the traditional working-class opposition. The activity of this new opposition is not, however, merely opposition, but is also the affirmation of a qualitatively different way of living. Against the system's postponement of *real* leisure and gratification, against its perpetuation of inhuman labor in the service of the ever further expansion of false needs, it affirms the right to enjoy a rational way of life on the basis of the present technological capacity to generate abundance while minimizing labor. It also testifies to the emergence of a new sensibility based on a singular sensitivity to the untruth of prevailing legitimations, to the costs, paid in terms of distorted individual and collective development, of the preservation of a society dominated by production for profits by competition for status and by the bureaucratization of every sphere of social life, and to the dangers of an order that of necessity increases aggression, both militarily and economically, instead of alleviating it. These costs are perceived as prohibitive in the light of a technological development that renders them no longer necessary.[40]

Although this new opposition is still only a relatively isolated minority, it achieves an importance far exceeding what is suggested by its numbers inasmuch as it suggests the possibility of a qualitative "rupture with the self-propelling conservative continuum of [repressive] needs" and understands, by virtue of its tendency to unite "instinctual and political rebellion," the possibility of liberation.[41] Within this new sensibility, the struggle against repressive society attains a "depth" dimension among still diffuse and atomized active minorities,

> which by virtue of their consciousness and their needs, function as potential catalysts of rebellion within the majorities to which . . . they belong. What appears as a surface phenomenon is indicative of basic tendencies which suggest not only different prospects of change, but also a depth and extent of change far beyond the expectations of traditional socialist theory.[42]

From this perspective, the diffusion of the negating forces and their displacement "from their traditional base among the underlying population," may be less a sign of their weakness in the face of the system's integrative capacity than simply the initial manifestations of a process signifying "the slow formation of a new base" and "the emergence of a new historical Subject of change, responding to the new objective conditions, with qualitatively different needs and aspirations." [43]

Notes

1. Reich, Preface to the third edition of *The Sexual Revolution*, p. xx.
2. Marcuse, Foreword to *Negations*, p. xi.
3. See Herbert Marcuse, *One-Dimensional Man: Studies in the Ideology of Advanced Industrial Society* (Boston, 1964); Jürgen Habermas, "Technology and Science as 'Ideology,'" in *Toward a Rational Society*; Trent Schroyer, "Toward a Critical Theory of Advanced Industrial Society," in Dreitzel, ed., *Recent Sociology No. 2*.
4. Lefebvre, *Everyday Life in the Modern World*, p. 60.
5. This phenomenon of artificially created scarcities under conditions of late capitalist production is perhaps most perceptively treated by André Gorz in *Strategy for Labor*, pp. 89–94.
6. R. Reiche, *Sexuality and Class Struggle*, p. 20.
7. T. W. Adorno, "Cultural Criticism and Society," in *Prisms* (London, 1967), p. 21.
8. Marcuse, "The Obsolescence of the Freudian Concept of Man," in *Five Lectures*, p. 47.
9. See Russ Jacoby, "The Politics of Subjectivity: Notes on Marxism, the Movement, and Bourgeois Society," *Telos*, no. 9 (Fall 1971), p. 120.
10. Horkheimer, "Authority and the Family," in *Critical Theory*, p. 114.
11. Marcuse, "The Obsolescence of the Freudian Concept of Man," in *Five Lectures*, p. 47.

12. Marcuse, "Freedom and Freud's Theory of Instincts," in ibid., p. 15.
13. Ibid.
14. Mitscherlich, *Society Without the Father*, p. 168.
15. See *One-Dimensional Man*, pp. 72–80; and David Ober, "On Sexuality and Politics in the Work of Herbert Marcuse," in Breines, ed., *Critical Interruptions*, pp. 101–35. A similar analysis has been worked out independently by Violette Morin and Joseph Majault, *Un mythe moderne: l'Érotisme* (Paris, 1964).
16. Marcuse, Preface to the Vintage Edition of *Eros and Civilization*, p. ix.
17. Ibid., p. x.
18. Ibid.
19. R. Reiche, *Sexuality and Class Struggle*, p. 17.
20. See the appendix entitled "Critique of Neo-Freudian Revisionism," *Eros and Civilization*, p. 218.
21. Herbert Marcuse, *Counter-Revolution and Revolt* (Boston, 1972), pp. 130–31.
22. Marcuse, *One-Dimensional Man*, p. 78.
23. Marcuse, "The Individual in the Great Society," in Bertram M. Gross, ed., *A Great Society?* (New York, 1968), p. 63.
24. Marcuse, "Aggressiveness in Advanced Industrial Society," in *Negations*, p. 257.
25. Ibid., p. 262.
26. Marcuse, "The Individual in the Great Society," p. 62.
27. Ibid., p. 63.
28. Ibid.
29. Sherry Weber, "Individuation as Praxis," in Breines, ed., *Critical Interruptions*, pp. 36–37.
30. See Lefebvre, *Critique de la vie quotidienne*, vol. II, pp. 307–13; Guy Debord, *Society of the Spectacle* (Detroit, 1970); and Norman Fruchter, "Movement Propaganda and the Culture of the Spectacle," *Liberation*, vol. 16, no. 3 (May 1971), pp. 4–17.
31. Hans Magnus Enzenburger, "Constituents of a Theory of the Media," *New Left Review*, no. 64 (November–December 1970), p. 24.

32. See Lefebvre, *Everyday Life in the Modern World*, pp. 78–80.
33. See André Gorz, *Strategy for Labor*; and James O'Connor, "The Fiscal Crisis of the State," *Socialist Revolution*, nos. 1 and 2.
34. William Leiss, "The Critical Theory of Society," in Breines, ed., *Critical Interruptions*, p. 99.
35. Enzenberger, "Constituents of a Theory of the Media," pp. 24–25.
36. Lefebvre, *Everyday Life in the Modern World*, p. 78.
37. Enzenberger, "Constituents of a Theory of the Media," p. 25.
38. Raoul Vaneigem, *Traité de savoir-vivre à l'usage des jeunes générations* (Paris, 1968), p. 30.
39. See Andrew Feenberg, "Technocracy and Rebellion," *Telos*, no. 8 (Summer 1971), p. 23.
40. See Jürgen Habermas, "Student Protest in the Federal Republic of Germany," in *Toward a Rational Society*, pp. 24, 29.
41. See Marcuse, Preface to the French edition of *One-Dimensional Man* (Paris, 1967).
42. Herbert Marcuse, *An Essay on Liberation* (Boston, 1969), p. 51.
43. Ibid., p. 52.

7

Toward a Method for the Revolutionary Reconstruction of Everyday Life

The reemergence of opposition within the advanced capitalist societies does not signify a return to the sort of class politics which characterized the pre-fascist era. It rather demands the elaboration of new forms of action and fresh strategic perspectives appropriate to the new forms of domination and new internal potentialities which characterize the latest stage in the development of capitalism. If the development of new techniques for the manipulation of behavior and the total administration of society has not, as we have suggested, been successful either in smothering the system's contradictions or in preventing the emergence of new and explosive forces of opposition, these new techniques have nevertheless altered decisively the basis for the development and organization of these potentially revolutionary forces in ways anticipated neither by traditional Marxian theory nor by its Reichian and Marcusean reformulations. These modifications pose a number of practical and theoretical problematics for the new oppositional forces which must be surmounted if they are to come to fruition in a new emancipatory praxis and which, if not resolved, will ultimately pose a threat to the very existence of these forces. The discussion to follow, without attempting to be systematic, will explore the nature of these problematics and

174

suggest some of the possible ways in which they may be resolved or overcome.

The first problematic facing the New Left is that of the necessity of bringing "nonrepressive" needs to consciousness and of liberating new desires within its own ranks and within the population as a whole. As the Frankfurt Marxists showed, bureaucratic, "consumer" capitalism, through its control over the formation and satisfaction of individual needs and through its elimination of all opportunities for autonomous individual development within its all-pervasive institutional apparatus, has achieved a degree of instinctive or primary integration among the dominated majority sufficient to repress its very capacity for subjective transcendence or spontaneous negation. Capitalist development thus reduces not only the environment of freedom and the "free space" necessary for the existence of individuality, but also the very desire and need for such an environment. Under these circumstances, "the individual and with him the rights and liberties of the individual is something that has still to be created, and that can be created only through the development of qualitatively different societal relations and institutions." [1] Although "all the material and intellectual forces [needed] for the realization of a free society are at hand," [2] and hence the advanced industrial societies are ripe for a revolution extending beyond the mere reorganization of production, a development and refinement is needed within the human psyche in order to bring it into correspondence with the level already reached by technological development and the potentialities contained within that development. There is a vicious circle: "The rupture with the self-propelling conservative continuum of needs must *precede* the revolution which is to usher in a free society, but such [a] rupture itself can be envisaged only in a revolution—a revolution which would be driven forward by the vital need to be freed from the administered comforts and the destructive productivity of the exploitative society." [3] A qualitative change must occur in the character of human needs, extending to the very depths of the biological infrastructure of the personality and demanding the transformation of the existing forms and contents of human life into qualitatively new ways of living. The pursuit of these ends—the liberation of previously suppressed human needs, desires, and possibilities and their coming-to-consciousness through a new sort of permanent cultural revolution—suggests the full extent and depth of the problematic confronting us. For the necessary "break in the historical continuum" which it implies must take place in the face of the following three difficulties:

> Firstly, that this break can only be theorized about in advance in categories, modes of thought and dreams bearing the hallmark of the existing society, and the oppression, exploitation and deprivation of liberty practiced in it; secondly, that it will have to be carried out by people who, though they suffer under this oppression, exploitation and deprivation of liberty, [though] they recognize them for what they are and want to do away with them, are also marked and maimed by them in their most minute feelings and habits; and thirdly, that the free society can only be built up on the basis of the maimed and fettered capacities of unfree societies. [4]

In the face of these obstacles, the project of "transforming life" is not going to be accomplished magically through a sort of poetic act, as the Surrealists believed. Such a cultural revolutionary project today will not and cannot simply unfold in the abstract, nor will it be achieved by the pure spontaneity of a practice of total negation and refusal. A practice which seeks the liberation of what has hitherto remained unconscious cannot itself be unconscious; on the contrary, it needs not less but more reflection and analysis than earlier revolutionary movements. Just as the capitalism of today has made the manipulation of individual behavior and need into a practical science, the cultural revolution which combats the system's repressive apparatus can only proceed on the basis of a critical revolutionary science which can master, both theoretically and practically, the dialectic of repression and integration through which the system infiltrates the terrain of everyday life. This means working out a multidimensional revolutionary project, building upon but going beyond the syntheses of Reich and Marcuse to incorporate the new complexities represented by current reality and by the oppositions to this reality.

Such a cultural revolutionary project, while having much in common with that of the Sex-Pol movement, nevertheless must begin by taking account of the new dimensions which have come to characterize the individual experience of oppression since Reich's day. Increasingly, the neuroses and Oedipal fixations he examined have been replaced by the contemporary syndromes of alienation: absurdity, nausea, superfluity, meaninglessness, schizophrenia, etc.[5] These new forms of psychological repression, like the older ones, serve to block the development of the individual's consciousness and hence of his/her capacity to act in a revolutionary manner, but their crippling effects are far more extensive and incalculably more severe. Accordingly, the cultural revolutionary project today must go beyond Reich's narrow emphasis on overcoming sexual repression; it must find methods of struggle which incorporate a total challenge to the way individual experience and authenticity are reduced by the repressive organization of everyday life. Given this "totalization" of alienation—this internalization of the repressive society outside—"a purely sexual counter-strategy or even a counter-strategy whose main bias is in this direction, is not by itself sufficient to wipe out exploitation."[6]

Such a project and such a strategy must begin at a much deeper and more fundamental level than Reich's did. For while the old Freudian ego produced by the patriarchal family was innately authoritarian and neurotic, at least it provided a subject for the Reichian project of overcoming the repressions which had deformed it. In the current stage of the development of repressive society, even the Self itself has become problematic—within this society each individual is nonidentical with her/himself. In place of the former unity of the Self there is only a succession or even a simultaneity of fragmentary perceptions in a fragmented environment. Under these circumstances, the unification of individual experiences within a framework capable of giving them meaning is rendered ever more difficult, if not impossible. The individual—unable to find a means of identifying him/herself within the framework of a segmented experience in which family, home, work, leisure, consumption, politics, etc., are all divided up—becomes ever farther removed from a dialectical comprehension of reality, ever farther removed from participation in creative praxis. Through a "systematization of confusion," as André Breton might have called it, the individual must discover the hidden principles of order underlying a chaotic existence.

An enormous amount of energy is available for this task, for the terms of survival defined by this society—the unconditional surrender of the self to the logic of bureaucratic power, the individual's acquiescence in her/his own dismemberment, the endless pursuit of pseudo-gratification by which the consumer is him/herself consumed—make everyday existence impossible to tolerate and lead a growing number of people into a total refusal of this reductive fragmentation. However, this refusal, and the aspirations toward subjective autonomy and toward a restoration of the essential wholeness of the self which it implies, come up against the total mobilization of the repressive society's formidable powers of containment and manipulation. Under these circumstances, they are foredoomed to failure unless they succeed from the very start in breaking free of the "blockage" imposed upon them by the system's success in maintaining the maximum isolation of the individual. Otherwise, the creative energies released by this refusal, confined to the monadic solitude of the individual's imagination, can only find an outlet in fantasy as the individual attempts to discover his/her lost "self" through an inward journey—a journey which leads to passivity or even madness. As Murray Bookchin has put it, to drop out in this sense is "to drop in." [7]

A practice capable of facilitating the individual's self-transformation while avoiding these pitfalls of solitude and self-destruction must thus be simultaneously subversive and therapeutic: it must be capable of undermining the triple pillars of hierarchy, specialization, and noncommunication by which the system maintains the individual in a state of passive subordination; and it must be capable of facilitating the crystallization of new, self-confident, and integrated personalities capable of subjective autonomy. Where is such a two-sided method of contestation and therapy to be found? It is in the search for an answer to this problematic that the developing practice of the New Left has led to the rediscovery, in the spontaneous capability of small groups, of a potential instrument of struggle which has not been given its full due since Proudhon's day. In its various contemporary manifestations (affinity groups, collectives, communes, micro-societies, consciousness-raising groups, etc.), the small group form has provided the New Left with an indispensable context *outside* the framework of the system's repressive apparatus within which to recreate the sort of "inter-human" milieu which alone can facilitate the difficult process of reconciling individual need and social purpose. As individuals escape the quiet desperation of their monadic existences and learn to identify with larger areas of social purpose, the practice of the group may nurture the emergence of the embryonic social self lying buried underneath the defenses (or to use Reich's term, the "character armor") which the individual has had to develop to survive in an atomized society. In addition to its therapeutic efficacy in the process of self-formation and development, the face-to-face group, inasmuch as it makes possible the tentative traversal of the gap separating the Self and its private world of needs, desires, and dreams, from the Other, also provides a medium for the accumulation of new types of inter-subjective experience (new modalities of human relationships, of emotionality, and of aesthetic perceptions). While these new relations cannot achieve full social expression within the existing society, they are an essential source for the transcendence of a false social consciousness and the formation of new utopian desires and demands. Finally, the practice of the group, by thus recreating the "free space" necessary for psychic growth, may enable the individual to become "conscious that social constructs experienced by the child as absolutes, since he has had no hand in shaping them, may in fact be altered by the impact of his will," [8] and thus to rediscover the innate creative initiative which has been suppressed since infancy.

Out of the formation and multiplication of such spontaneous groupings of people, whose aim is to overcome the atomization and reduction of everyday existence through new experiences of collective solidarity, we can discern the creation of a micro-political base for the formation of a new revolutionary culture and consciousness.* The search for

---

* At the same time, the undoubted efficacy of the small group in these respects should not be allowed to obscure the recognition not only of the limitations of small-group practice but also of potential abuse of this form for repressive and manipulative ends—a recuperation which ought to be obvious in the light of the close connections between the development of various schools of group dynamics and the practice of industrial relations.[9] More specifically, even in France, where an explicitly "leftist" group

unalienated interpersonal relations and new ways of living which gives the life of these groups its experimental character not only generates a new sensitivity to the atrophied modes of experiencing interaction and the administered modes of life and labor which define the existing macro-political order, but also gives rise to new conflicts and contradictions within that order. Perhaps the most typical of these new antagonisms is the contradiction between the aspiration to subjective autonomy in the decisions that affect one's life, and the necessity of adapting oneself to the demands of bureaucratic super-organizations, of accepting the limitations placed on personal initiative and responsibility by the restrictive role-definitions of these large-scale institutions. The rejection of this hierarchical control found its programmatic expression in the American New Left's principle of "participatory democracy," both as a method of self-organization within the movement and as the basis for a utopian project aimed at transforming society as a whole. Alongside and underneath this conflict, however, there emerge others, even more fundamental: between psychic needs and practical demands, between the imaginary and the real, between thought and feeling, between desire and realization, etc. Out of the perception of the contrast between the extreme humiliation, boredom, and enforced passivity of everyday life, the result of its subordination to hierarchical power, and a develop-

---

dynamics or "psychosociology" of Marxist inspiration has developed and has taken as its project the "leavening" of social tensions,[10] the role of such interventions as a means of revealing contradictions and unleashing contestations has at best proved ambiguous. In particular, as Joseph Gabel argues in his article, "Marxisme et dynamique de groupe" in *Arguments* (see n. 10), such a group dynamics, unless it is situated in the framework of a much wider critique and practice than that of the small group, inevitably runs the risk, despite its intentions, of promoting a new false consciousness —that is, of suggesting "the possibility of a non-political transcendence of capitalist reification."

ment of society's productive capacity which renders that power anachronistic, there arises a profound need for the social expression of creativity, for the recovery of all the creative richness and energy lost through the impoverishment and over-organization of everyday life.

In the face of the quasi-imperialist logic by which the bureaucratic system of controlled consumption has extended itself—not only spatially through the unification of the world market, but also through the colonization of every sphere of daily life—the attempt to transform the new affinity groups into "liberated enclaves" or counter-societies (rural communes, therapeutic communities, etc.) that seek a partial or localized transcendence of alienation and reification are as easily contained or consumed by the larger social order as are attempts at individual escape. Nothing testifies to the quixotic nature of this endeavor better than the self-destructive and regressive implosion that has characterized the disillusioning history of the so-called Woodstock Nation. In contrast, if the quite real and fundamental utopian spirit which underlay the early years of the youth culture is to escape the "recuperations" * prepared for it by the system's repressive apparatus and its pervasive "spectacle," it must actualize itself through a new praxis aimed not at the *evasion* of everyday life, but at its *transformation*.

Such a praxis must be total in the sense that it seeks the reappropriation of everything that the system takes away. It is men and women who have, through their activity, produced the system. But as a result of the appropriation of this activity by hierarchical power, they now experience its

---

* The notion of *recuperation*, first introduced by the Situationists, refers to the manner in which the repressive system seeks to neutralize or contain the attacks launched against it by *absorbing* them into the "spectacle" or by *projecting* its own meanings and goals onto these oppositional activities.

product (that is, the product of their own creativity) as an alien force (a "given" system of constraints embodied in ideas, in language, in institutions whose origins have been forgotten) in which they cannot recognize themselves. This praxis seeks to destroy all the constraints imposed on the creative self-activity of men and women by this world of alien objects and reified forms, while simultaneously creating a new world in which these men and women can recognize themselves—a world in which the realm of the "given" is encountered only as the "free gift" of past human creativity and as the precondition for their own future creativity. Such an assertion of the claims of human creativity against everything that degrades it should not be used to justify the sort of abstract maximalism or pure contestation which assumes a totally open-ended view of the possibilities available to revolutionary practice. If everything is possible, then nothing is possible. Such a false consciousness, born of a legitimate fear of co-optation or containment, tends in practice toward a nihilistic refusal which at best may temporarily disrupt the routine of everyday life without allowing any real expression of creativity. If allowed to run its course, it logically ends in self-destruction: it points toward a confrontation with power which it cannot win since it takes place on power's own terms and terrain. If these twin pitfalls of integration and self-destruction are to be avoided through the elaboration of a method for the conscious transformation of everyday life, what is required is a new sort of practical *and* theoretical intervention which proceeds by uniting conceptual analysis with what Henri Lefebvre calls "socio-analytical experience" *—a sort of continuous action-

---

* More generally, according to Lefebvre, such a socio-analytical practice presupposes "interventions into an actual situation, a community's everyday life." In particular, "the socio-analytical intervention *dissociates* into place and time the bearings of the situation, combined as they are with

critique aimed at even the most trivial details of daily life. Such a critique aims, first of all, at unveiling, through analysis and through practical exploration, the specific constraints and alternatives which define the dialectic of possibility-impossibility at any particular moment. Such a critique of everyday life, if it is to be carried on under the current conditions constituted by the "totalization" of alienation and "the fact of the integration of the conscious and the unconscious and the latter's externalization," suggests the need for what Jeremy Shapiro has described as "a psycho-analysis of the external world." [12] In other words, it would attempt to do for all the other institutional contexts within which everyday life is organized what Freud and later Reich began to do for the patriarchal family, and to relate each of these various interpersonal milieux to the social totality within which they arise and which is, in turn, conditioned by their cumulative or "over-determined" effect.

Accordingly, this "socio-analysis" of everyday life must, like psychoanalysis itself, proceed simultaneously on several discrete levels. First of all, it begins with the recognition that in a society whose bureaucratic apparatus has so profoundly invaded even the deepest roots of the individual experience, the projects of self-transformation inaugurated within face-to-face groups can progress only to the extent that they succeed in simultaneously subverting the institutional contexts in which they have arisen. This means analyzing, discrediting, and disassembling these institutions in such a way as to undermine their apparent universality and rationality and, by thus stripping away the mask of reification and mystification, to reveal their real origins as the objectification of human purpose and activity. This means that even before hierarchical power can be encountered and contested on the

---

false evidence; it [thus] *associates* experiences that were previously foreign to it, and then proceeds by induction and transduction." [11]

political or economic level, it must be attacked in the realm of the social imagination, of what the Situationists call "the spectacle"—the systematic organization of appearances through which the domination of hierarchical power is expressed by the closure of the fields of socially available perception, extending from the definition of the possible and the impossible, the useful and the useless, the good and the bad, to that of the rational and irrational, the future and the past. This perception is carried in the whole web of social relations in the form of the objective future which determines their persistence and resistance to change. It is, however, most fundamentally expressed on the specific level of language and communications, and, on this level, through the repressive society's incorporation of fantasy, of the imagination, and of the aesthetic into the spectacle. It follows that a revolutionary coming-to-consciousness aimed at the total transformation of everyday life must begin by opening up the field of possibility through a recovery of this realm of imagination and fantasy and its translation into social practice. As Paul Cardan has observed, it is mistaken to believe that "the imaginary" comes into play only as the result of a failure to solve "real" problems. The distinction is utterly false, for when such "real" problems are solved, it is only because people have exercised their "imaginary" powers. Moreover, the very identification of things *as* "real problems" is contingent on the specific "imaginary" complex that defines a particular time or place.[13] There is nothing "God-given" about reality; but the imagination that is at work in it is concealed from us by the false images of the spectacle.

It is in the light of this need to cross the boundary between the possible and impossible, the real and the imaginary, that it becomes possible to grasp the significance of some of the new forms of struggle whose spontaneous emergence has characterized the development of the New Left. The notion of "contestation," for example, may be seen primarily as a method for "unlocking" the barriers erected by the spectacle against social expression, imagination, and communication. By introducing "free speech" and uninterrupted dialogue, by initiating tension and disorder, participation and festivity, these actions (originating in the initiative of active minorities within the universities, but subsequently spreading to other institutional contexts as well) attack not so much hierarchical power itself as its pseudo-universal mythologies—its attempt to insulate itself by representing the degradations it imposes on society as "normal," eternal, natural verities, as immutable facts of life.

Similarly, the related conception of "exemplary actions" constitutes an original attempt to confront the problem of diffusing revolutionary themes and aspirations in a society where the manipulative use of the mass media tends to transform any action into a neutral spectacle. The exemplary action fights this new kind of censorship with a symbolic act of liberation which rejects "the rules of the game," which challenges the whole logic of the system. Such actions, while launched within a particular, localized institutional context, seek to transcend their parochial origins through their symbolic efficacy in conveying to other groups, who can identify their own circumstances with those of the original actors, the secret of how to take matters into their own hands in the cause of their own liberation.

Finally, and in this regard with only ambiguous success, the struggles launched by the new oppositional groupings provide a tentative idea of the methods by which the fragmentation and disinfection of language, in the interests of concealing and legitimating hierarchical power and disarming its political opponents, might be overcome. One aspect of such a method for liberating language is the reappropriation of the meanings which have been taken over by the apparatus in the interests of power, reduced to mere signals for the transmission of orders from above, and reimposed on the masses—who thus become mere *receivers* of these orders. How such a reconquest of language might take place—through a redistribution of the power of expression to those from whom it has been taken away, or to whom it had never been granted at all—was suggested by the May–June events of 1968 in France. The institutional crisis initiated by the student contestation was accompanied by a parallel breakdown in the structures of repressive communication through which hierarchical power imposes its political predefinitions and official symbols on the language of public life. Within the void created by the absence of these legitimating symbols, a battle broke out over the rules of interpretation by which the symbolic order was to be reconstructed, a battle which was fought out each morning when groups of people throughout Paris would gather in the streets and theaters to discuss the meaning of the preceding night's events. The Latin Quarter, for example, became a vast forum in which "speech," suppressed during the preceding period of repression and stability, burst forth "to take," in the words of Henri Lefebvre, "a devastating revenge on the constraints of written language." [14] To be sure, this inflation of language was often demagogic or puerile, and, on the theoretical level, poetically metaphysical, but it did suggest the possibility of a unification between the language of critical consciousness and the language of action which would permit an insurrectional seizure of the power of the word—the power of the intellect and the power of communication—by those to whom it had hitherto been denied.[15] *

---

* More generally, as the Situationists have pointed out, the destruction of the repressive order requires the simultaneous transcendence of the language which conceals and guarantees it. "The criticism of the dominant language, its *détournement*, is in the process of becoming the permanent practice of new revolutionary theory." In particular, "because every new interpretation is called misinterpretation by the authorities," they intend "to legitimize misinterpretation and denounce the imposture of the guaranteed interpretation handed out by the power structure." [16]

At the same time, the cultural revolutionary process which has been launched by these actions cannot remain solely within the sphere of the imaginary. This cultural revolution, as Peter Schneider has pointed out, "is no aesthetic ersatz for revolution; it is not a putsch in a museum, nor an attack on a park, nor a scandal in a theater—such applications amount to leaving culture in the ghetto to which capitalism condemned it in the first place." [17] The new utopian culture which is the object of the revolutionary reconstruction of everyday life is not something which can first be imagined in its entirety and *then* created; it must be created and imagined at the same time. This requires not only the occupation of "mental space," but of a "space" which is material as well as symbolic. The liberation of language from all that has degraded it is necessary and fundamental, but it is not sufficient. The new images of utopia cannot bear fruit unless they materialize themselves by actually entering into the social division of labor. Otherwise, the process of disalienation through refusal and contestation, street actions and festivities, will affect only the "spectacular" images of power, leaving the summits of bureaucratic power and their roots in the economic base undisturbed. As enthusiasm ebbs and spontaneity reaches its limits, these pillars of order will become the axes around which the structures of everyday life will tend to resolidify. A cultural revolutionary project which aims at the actual transformation and not just the suspension of everyday existence must be capable of countering such attempts to impose the reorganization of everyday life from above with a concrete project of its own aimed at reconstructing social life from below.

The specifically utopian functions of cultural contestation must be supplemented by a strategy of anti-institutional struggle, and "the long march through the institutions" recognized as the only road to the realization of the new utopian culture. In general terms, this means a fusion of the cultural and political revolutions into a new conception of politics, within a struggle "to extend the community's realm of choice and decision over the entirety of social life in the interests of needs that do not require domination." [18] What emerges is a new model of the revolutionary process, simultaneously involving destruction and creation, negation and affirmation, and uniting individual self-realization with social consciousness. Characterizing this new praxis is a panorama of practical-theoretical development that can be described as follows: it begins with the individual's personal experience of oppression and of the fragmentation of experience which makes authentic experience impossible for her or him; it leads from the discovery of this alienation to the individual's refusal of it through a process which is best described as the *politicization of oneself* and which aims at a retotalization of the individual's experience; it develops further through the individual's collision with the inertia of an oppressive social reality in his or her search for authenticity; with this recognition of the social sources of the individual's malaise, it leads to the inauguration of a radical contestation of existing institutions on the level of everyday life carried out by small groups and collectives, and extended through their spontaneous multiplication as micro-social centers of resistance; it finally attains a truly social dimension, uniting the struggle for the creation of a new self with the struggle for the creation of a new society, through the emergence of new needs and capacities for self-organization within broad sectors of the population and the attempt on the part of these groups to engender the creation of new forms of self-management (or, as the French call it, *autogestion*) throughout every sphere of social activity. Thus, from all sides, the eruption of localized centers of contestation and the further politicization of these contesting currents lead to the demand for a new collective self-regulation of life, for a generalization of self-management throughout society. In this sense, self-management becomes both the principal means and method for the reconstruction of everyday life and, simultaneously, the principal goal of this reconstruction.

> Self-management portends the surge through the breach of a process extending over the whole of society. It would be wrong to confine this process to the management of economic affairs (enterprises, branches of industry, etc.). Self-management implies a social *pedagogy*. It presupposes a new social practice at all stages and levels. This process involves the shattering of bureaucracy and centralized state management [and] implies the establishment at the base [of society] of a complex network of active bodies. [Its] practice and theory modify the classic concept of [representative democracy]. The many interests of the base must be present, and not merely 'represented' or handed over to delegates who become divorced from the base. Effective self-management and participation cannot be separated from a "system" of direct democracy akin more to a continuous and continuously renewed movement deriving its organizational capacities from within itself, than to a formal "system." Relations change at all levels. The old relations between those who are active and those who are passive, between the rulers and the ruled, between decisions and frustrations, between subjects and objects—all these are dissolved.[19]

Such a notion of generalized self-management thus provides the basis for a strategy of "dual power" which would deprive the centralized power of its role as the "repressive unifier" of society by instituting new forms of everyday life, of working life, of "the festival," of collective self-expression and uninstitutionalized dialogue.* Inasmuch as it places the

---

* Naturally, the crystallization of such a "counter-hegemonic force" out of a strategy of dual power implies a subversion of the societal apparatus of communication.[20] The centrally controlled, pyramidal organization of media, disseminating messages from above to fragmented mass individuals,

existing society as a whole in question, it is possible to discern a new contradiction opening up between the general extension of such demands for and attempts to implement self-management, on the one hand, and the existing forms of state power and institutional authority, on the other. At the same time, the struggle for the creation of such a system of dual power as a method of revolutionary struggle leading to the total liberation of everyday life faces certain obstacles and raises certain new problems of theory and practice. For self-management is a hollow slogan if it is taken in isolation from the concrete problems it raises and abstracted from a concrete theoretical project. It only becomes meaningful when its social and political content is placed within the context of a revolutionary program for the whole of society and an all-inclusive strategy which adapts this program to the actual social forces which are presently in motion.

Herein lies the final and in many respects the most formidable problematic facing the movement. For whereas the project of restoring a repressive social order from above finds its social basis in a small but highly unified minority, the demand for a revolutionary reconstruction of everyday life, for generalized self-management, has a potential social basis which, while incomparably broader, is at the same time highly dispersed and atomized. The reasons for this are

---

must be replaced by decentralized, "horizontal" lines of communication in which each group or individual is no longer a mere passive receiver, but a potential transmitter of information. In this regard, Vaneigem has suggested that the very "complexity of communication techniques (which might appear to be a pretext for the survival or return of specialists) is just what makes possible the continuous control of delegates [to revolutionary assemblies] by the base—the confirmation, correction, rejection of their decisions at all levels." In short, the organization of dual power demands that the various base groups appropriate for their use all the necessary means of communications—radio/TV transmitters, telephones, duplicators, etc.[21]

complicated, but in general appear to be a consequence of the forms of politicization through which the various currents of contestation have necessarily developed in order to oppose a capitalism which has unified itself to the extent that its domination is becoming increasingly universal and which is, at the same time, tending toward totalitarian self-regulation. In the face of a worldwide organization of repression and its equally pervasive "spectacle" which tend toward the obliteration of all difference and all autonomy through the universal extension of commodity relations, the reemergence of opposition has had necessarily to begin with a return to the basic and the specific, with the reassertion of differentiation—that is, with explosive contestations launched outside of or beneath the "apparatus" and conducted in the name of racial, cultural, linguistic, and sexual particularisms.

The development of revolutionary movements, both in the Third World and among the colonized minorities of the metropolitan countries, thus confronts Marxist theory with the paradox of revolutionary struggles against the whole imperialist system which are fought, not in the name of proletarian internationalism, but in the name of national independence and ethnic solidarity.[22] In this way, black people, by pursuing their independence in the name of "negritude" and the creation of "black power," turn what was a symbol of inferiority into a fund of positive values and a potent instrument of struggle—the assertion of a new revolutionary identity and its actualization in the formation of new (and usually exclusivist) revolutionary organizations. The subsequent politicization and self-affirmation first of youth and then of women in the industrial West has taken place through the same process of refusing pseudo-universal ideologies in the name of revolutionary particularisms. All three groups begin their search for new revolutionary identities by differentiating themselves from the image of a Western civilization—first elaborated according to aristocratic criteria and then reproduced for and "consumed" by the adult, bourgeois, Euro-American male—in whose formation they had hitherto participated only peripherally and marginally and hence in which they can recognize themselves only as "objects," never as "subjects." In opposition to this dispossession of their historical existence, to this reduction of their experience, the conceptions of "youth culture" and "feminism"—like those of "negritude" and "black nationalism"—assert the desire of these groups to become the makers of their own history and, in doing so, to become modes of humanity in general from which all possible human values can be drawn. The new identities formed in this way provide a matrix through which the bridge between the Self and the Other is crossed and the possibilities of identification with the larger social totality are experienced in terms of a sphere of shared interest and action. Moreover, by uniting oppressed groups at the level of their total oppression, the new collective identities lay the basis for a "global" contestation—for a total attack on a specific complex of oppression which serves to articulate a universal human predicament and project as encountered in each group's particular condition.

At the same time, this sort of "totalist" practice which expresses a protest against all oppressive conditions in the form of a demand for complete liberation, for the overthrow of the whole of capitalist society, remains fatally marked by the incoherence of its birth and the "monadic" fragmentation of its development. The attempt to reconstitute the "total" man or woman as a prelude to total confrontation with power, if undertaken by a partial social force in isolation from other such forces, leads almost inevitably to a process of organizational and linguistic encapsulation of the contesting current within micro-societies or countercultures—the fragmentation of the revolution being seen as the price that must be paid to overcome the fragmentation of individual experience and to reestablish communication. (For example, in the women's movement, a period during which women work exclusively with each other in overcoming their old roles and forging new identities is usually seen as a precondition for any sexually integrated revolutionary movement. Without this separate experience of consciousness-raising, it is argued, the old patterns of domination and submission would simply reassert themselves.) Given the current development of the technological basis of modern society to the point where its structure and the problems it poses are increasingly international or even universal in character and hence demand "planetary" or universal solutions, the realization of claims for generalized self-management within the restricted definitions of such partial social forces could only constitute a self-management of exploitation and confusion. Inasmuch as these claims are everywhere launched in isolation, not only is their ultimate realization precluded, but even their immediate survival is threatened. For any struggle—the student movement, for example—which depicts itself as revolutionary and total while in fact remaining partial and isolated, in effect can encounter only the strongest, not the weakest, link of the system. These partial contestations are thus doubly threatened: first, they mobilize all of the forces of the international repressive apparatus against what is really only part of the forces opposing this apparatus; and second, they risk alienating other groups within the constellation of contestation—some black and women's liberation struggles, for instance, tend to demand a liberation in one sphere of society which is denied to the oppressed masses as a whole in other spheres (leading, to take an example, to the resistance of the white working class to the demands of black workers). A perspective which includes only the liberation of a part within the whole can only appear to those outside it as a liberation to be purchased at their expense.

If the new revolutionary currents are to surmount this

impasse, it is crucial that they transcend the limitations of their particularity and work out, in practice and in theory, a new, unifying perspective capable of linking partial struggles and specific oppressions to their common objective roots and of joining them within a totalizing revolutionary project. There is no simple formula for creating such a strategy and project. In the old classical Marxist perspective, the division of the world into two classes, whose antagonisms would increase to the eventual point of revolutionary rupture, made it possible to offer one of these classes—the workers—a total vision of the world and a utopian project which served them as a continual source of hope and a powerful incentive to revolt. Today, we no longer have a generalized conception of the oneness of civilization capable of inspiring a unified revolutionary subject to revolt and of guiding its struggles. Rather, we have a many-sided revolutionary praxis, carried on simultaneously at every level and consisting of a multiplicity of utopian projects and separate inclinations, each tending toward the universal and each creating, in the process of its struggle, new institutions, new identities, and new organs of direct democracy. Given this heterogeneous experience of struggle, the revolutionary project cannot begin from *a priori* formulae, but must be developed through a continual process of synthesis, fermentation, and dialectical totalization.

The character of such a totalization is determined by the constant effort to take account of the opposing requirements of unity and multiplicity, of real and non-derivative antagonisms, in order to effect their unification within a project for the transformation of society as a whole—a project which neither reduces coherence to the partial nor is itself reducible to a partial point of view. Totality, if it is to be devoid of all totalitarian tendencies, can only be viewed as a *process* moving in the direction of the reconstruction of society on a new, planetary base.[23] Although only the barest outlines of such a new process of the universal, horizontal socialization of humanity are visible, one possible direction in which it may be proceeding is through what Jacques Berque has called "the modalization of man," [24] through a sort of universal syncretism on the cultural level (the reciprocal exchange of elements originating in the black experience and those original to the counterculture of white youth—say, of blues and acid rock represented at one pole by Jimi Hendrix and at the other by the Stones—is a fairly paradigmatic example of this process, which seems to be assuming planetary dimensions). Perhaps, through an immense cross-fertilization of cultures, of modalities of experience, of life-styles, etc., a new civilization may be in the act of being born which will, in the wake of the forced homogenization of life by the quasi-imperialist logic of hierarchical power, recreate on a planetary scale what Lévi-Strauss has called that "certain *optimum* of diversity" that previously defined human societies and which, according to him, they can neither go *beyond* nor *below* without being endangered.

By way of conclusion, I would simply like to emphasize, in the light of what I have just said, that the concept of cultural revolution should not mean losing sight of older projects, such as those of economic and political revolution. The struggle for a cultural revolution, far from being something which replaces earlier conflicts such as the class struggle, is meaningful only as a *cumulative* project—a project which incorporates into itself all the unrealized or incompletely realized liberatory aims of the earlier struggles, thus giving a new power of expression to all those revolutionary needs and energies that had previously always remained more or less implicit or submerged. What today is called cultural revolution is none other than the totalization and reinvigoration of all the liberatory endeavors launched by past generations of revolutionaries, as well as of the novel problems posed by the contemporary world crisis, all of which have been taken up in a more or less subjective manner by the struggles we associate with the idea of a New Left and posed by it on a level which is still largely confined to the aesthetic or "imaginary" realm. The problems are thus cumulative, and because they are cumulative they demand that we continually develop new hypotheses that take account of their complexity. For inasmuch as these struggles for a new world continue to progress, they will, with each step forward, also confront us with new exigencies and new problems. These include, among others, those of reappropriating the integrity of our individual, social, and planetary dimensions: the individual, through the release of hitherto suppressed creative needs and passions; the social, through the liberation of language, the revival of a collective spirit of festivity and free play and the reassertion of all those modes of community and communion which have hitherto been suppressed by the reductive logic of hierarchical power; the planetary, through the expansion of reciprocal exchange between civilizations and modes of experience which have hitherto been subordinated, ignored, or evaded, and which will become the new modalities for the emergence of the men and women of the future. If we are to carry on with our cultural revolutionary project, we must continually remain open to new experiences and unforeseen problems and we must continually extend our practice toward the realization of a collective life in which everyone would exercise all their creative faculties and in which all the valences—individuals, social, planetary—which would constitute such a new civilization in all its plenitude would be liberated.

Notes

1. Marcuse, Preface to the Vintage edition of *Eros and Civilization*, p. viii.

198   *Bruce Brown*

2. Marcuse, "The End of Utopia," in *Five Lectures*, p. 64.
3. Marcuse, *An Essay on Liberation*, pp. 18–19.
4. R. Reiche, *Sexuality and Class Struggle*, pp. 165–66.
5. Jeremy Schapiro, "One-Dimensionality: The Universal Semiotic of Technological Experience," in Breines, ed., *Critical Interruptions*, p. 175.
6. R. Reiche, *Sexuality and Class Struggle*, p. 25.
7. Murray Bookchin, "Desire and Need," *Anarchos*, no. 1 (February 1968), p. 40.
8. George Benello, "Group Organization and Socio-Political Structure," in Benello and Roussopoulos, eds., *The Case for Participatory Democracy* (New York, 1971), p. 41.
9. See Loren Baritz, *The Servants of Power* (New York, 1965).
10. See G. Lapassade, *Groupes, Organisations et Institutions* (Paris, 1967); and the special issue of *Arguments* entitled "Vers une psycho-sociologie politique," vol. 6, nos. 25–26 (1962).
11. Marcuse, *Everyday Life in the Modern World*, p. 188–89.
12. Schapiro, "One-Dimensionality," pp. 179–80.
13. See Paul Cardan, "Marxisme et théorie révolutionnaire," *Socialisme ou Barbarie*, no. 30 (March–April 1965), pp. 63–64.
14. Lefebvre, *The Explosion*, p. 119.
15. See Horia Bratu, "Happenings for Real," *Partisan Review* (Fall 1969), pp. 534–35; and Peter Brook, "The Fourth World," in ibid. (Winter 1969), pp. 34–38.
16. Mustapha Khayati, "Les mots captifs," *Internationale Situationniste*, no. 8 (Spring 1968).
17. Peter Schneider, "Die Phantasie im Spätkapitalismus und die Kulturrevolution," *Kursbuch*, no. 16 (1969), p. 3.
18. Schapiro, "One-Dimensionality," pp. 181–82.
19. Lefebvre, *The Explosion*, pp. 85–86.
20. See Enzensberger, "Constituents of a Theory of the Media," pp. 25–26.
21. See Vaneigem, "Avis aux civilisés relativement à l'autogestion generalisée," *Internationale Situationniste*, no. 12 (1969), pp. 74–79.

22. See the third section of Edgar Morin's *Introduction à une politique de l'homme* (Paris, 1965).

23. Lefebvre, *The Explosion*, pp. 127–29.

24. See Jacque Berque, "Quelques problèmes de la décolonisation," *L'Homme et la Société,* no. 5.

Name Index